SEXUALITY
After Spinal
Cord Injury

D0887342

SEXUALITY
After Spinal Cord Injury

Answers to Your Questions

by
Stanley H. Ducharme, Ph.D.
Boston University School of Medicine
and
Kathleen M. Gill, Ph.D.
Harvard University School of Medicine

·P·A·U·L·H·
BROOKES
PUBLISHING C°

Baltimore • London • Toronto • Sydney

Paul H. Brookes Publishing Co.
Post Office Box 10624
Baltimore, Maryland 21285-0624

Copyright © 1997 by Paul H. Brookes Publishing Co., Inc.
All rights reserved.

Typeset by Maple Vail Composition Service, Binghamton, New York.
Manufactured in the United States of America by
The Maple Press Co., York, Pennsylvania.

Funding for the original handbook provided by the Education and Training Foundation, Paralyzed Veterans of America.

The suggestions in this book are not intended as a substitute for professional medical consultation. The authors and publisher disclaim any lia-
bility arising directly or indirectly from the use of this book.

Library of Congress Cataloging-in-Publication Data
Ducharme, Stanley H.
    Sexuality after spinal cord injury : answers to your
    questions / by Stanley H. Ducharme and Kathleen M.
    Gill.
        p.   cm.
    Includes bibliographical references and index.
    ISBN 1-55766-265-7
1. Spinal cord—Wounds and injuries—Patients—Sexual
behavior—Miscellanea.   2. Sex instruction for the physically handicapped—Miscellanea.   I. Gill, Kathleen
M.   II. Title.
RD594.3.D83   1997
613.9'5'0873–dc20   96-22886
                                                        CIP

British Library Cataloguing-in-Publication data are available from the
British Library.

Contents

List of Illustrations vii
About the Authors viii
Foreword   *Sandra S. Cole* ix
Preface.. xii
Acknowledgments xv

Introduction 1

Introduction to spinal cord injury, male sexual anatomy and sexual health, female sexual anatomy and sexual health, the phases of sexual arousal

1   Rehabilitation and Community Integration.............................. 17

In the rehabilitation center, depression and anger, when to resume sex, sex in the rehabilitation center, medical professionals, caregivers

2   Emotional and Social Concerns 31

Body image and self-esteem, dating, relationships, sex, marriage, growing older

3   Physical Aspects... 71

Smoking, drugs, erections, masturbation, vibrators, orgasm, bladder/bowel issues, intercourse, time and place, positions

4   Fertility, Feminine Hygiene, and Parenting............................ 119

Men's fertility, ejaculation, birth control, menstruation, women's fertility, pregnancy, parenting

5   Sexually Transmitted Diseases and Future Research............. 141

AIDS and other diseases, safe sex, high-risk sex, new research

Appendix A   Glossary... 151

Appendix B   Resources 165

Appendix C   Independent Living Centers in the
             United States and Canada....................................... 167

Appendix D   Statewide Independent Living Councils.............. 215

Index 235

List of Illustrations

1. The spinal cord and corresponding nerves................................... 2

2. The male sexual anatomy.. 6

3. The female sexual anatomy 9

4. Piston vacuum erection system (courtesy of Mentor
    Urology)... 83

5. Response battery-powered vacuum erection system
    (courtesy of Mentor Urology).. 84

6. Alpha I inflatable penile implant (courtesy of Mentor
    Urology)... 86

7. Acu-form bendable penile implant (courtesy of Mentor
    Urology)... 87

8. Penile injection system.. 90

9. Vibrator adapted for an individual with limited hand use............ 94

10. Birth control options... 125

About the Authors

Stanley H. Ducharme, Ph.D., is a clinical/health psychologist on the medical staff at Boston Medical Center. He is also Clinical Professor of Rehabilitation Medicine and Assistant Professor of Urology at Boston University School of Medicine. Dr. Ducharme is editor of the *Journal of Sexuality and Disability* and is a member of the board of directors of the Education and Training Foundation of the Paralyzed Veterans of America.

Kathleen M. Gill, Ph.D., is a lecturer in psychology at Harvard University School of Medicine, Boston, Massachusetts. She is also a clinical psychologist in the Sexual Function Clinic at Lahey-Dartmouth Medical Center in Burlington, Massachusetts. Dr. Gill is a founding clinical fellow in The American Academy of Clinical Sexologists and a diplomate/clinical supervisor for The American Board of Sexology. She publishes regularly in the area of sexuality and maintains a private practice in sex therapy.

Foreword

In the early 1970s, materials regarding the sexual concerns and sexual happiness of people with disabilities began to emerge in the literature. Before that time, the topic of sexual health was rarely mentioned by professionals when discussing concerns and health care issues that accompanied a spinal cord injury trauma. This was partly due to a lack of information in the medical world and partly due to the discomfort and hesitancy of medical professionals in speaking forthrightly about sexuality.

Now, with the assistance and contribution of people with spinal cord injuries, many valuable materials have been developed. Although the literature is not exactly robust, it contains helpful information for professionals working with people with spinal cord injuries and their families. There are still, however, very few publications that directly address the concerns of people with spinal cord injuries themselves. Since 1970, only a few books, scattered newsletters, and publications have emerged, along with a small number of videotapes of an instructional and explicit nature. These tapes depict a range of options for sexual behavior and contain interviews with individuals and couples speaking about their personal lives. They are welcome contributions to information resources.

I was very pleased to learn of the availability of *Sexuality After Spinal Cord Injury: Answers to Your Questions.* As I reviewed the contents of this book, I noted its comprehensive scope—addressing single individuals, couples in relationships, individuals in between relationships, those planning on establishing relationships, and those who are parenting. Friends and intimates of people with spinal cord injuries will also benefit from learning specific information about sexuality and spinal cord injury.

It is well known that information can dispel myths, remove anxiety regarding sexuality, and positively influence one's self-confidence and self-esteem. A beneficial feature of this handbook is that it delivers current and accurate information in a succinct, straightforward fashion. The question-and-answer format is not overly elaborate, confusing, or filled with medical jargon. Questions are given careful and respectful consideration; education and recommendations are provided. All of us like to be self-reliant and confident about our personal worth and abilities. This handbook provides a means of independently gaining information and assists in restoring dignity and privacy and reducing anxiety for individuals with legitimate and reasonable questions.

A broad spectrum of topics covers various circumstances that affect individuals, couples, and families. These include ethics, personal boundaries, predictable problematic situations, and positive recommendations and solutions. The book particularly focuses on recognizing emotional issues that can be triggered by the presence of a spinal cord injury and on the need for effective communication skills with one's partner. I was pleased to see that both male and female issues were addressed. It has been my experience that very few publications have focused on answering questions that women, in particular, might have regarding sexual health. Helpful information and recommendations dealing with fertility, technology, pregnancy prevention, and sexual function are certainly a welcome addition to the resources available. Practical advice regarding daily living and strong recommendations for "smart sex" and the avoidance of sexually transmitted diseases are valuable. This handbook also answers questions about where to go for help and how to select the appropriate kind of help.

I am sure *Sexuality After Spinal Cord Injury* will prove to be an excellent and useful resource. The compilation of information reflects the high quality and vast experience of the authors and their years of service and education regarding the sexual health concerns of those with spinal cord injuries. This is an important publication for active individuals in contemporary times.

I am enthusiastic and pleased to have a small part in this important project, appropriately sponsored and funded by the Education and Training Foundation of the Paralyzed Veterans of America. I was flooded with memories of the first publication project in which I was involved and which pioneered a focus on explicit information and education regarding spinal cord injury and sexuality. It was the Paralyzed Veterans of America who funded that first publication entitled *Sexual Options for Paraplegics and*

Quadriplegics (Mooney, Cole, & Chilgren, 1975). Their ongoing commitment to the promotion of sexual health and happiness of those with spinal cord injuries is commendable.

Sandra S. Cole, Ph.D.
Professor of Physical Medicine and Rehabilitation
University of Michigan Medical Center
Ann Arbor, Michigan

REFERENCE

Mooney, T., Cole, T., & Chilgren, R. (1975). *Sexual options for paraplegics and quadriplegics.* Boston: Little, Brown.

Preface

Back in the late 1970s, a group of us in Boston got together and began to look into questions of sexuality for people with physical disabilities, especially people with spinal cord injuries. Some of us had disabilities, while others were working in rehabilitation hospitals with people who had disabilities. Between us, we pooled our various experiences and resources to develop training programs that attempted to address the most common—and common-sensical—questions that came up about sex:

- "Can I ever make love again?" asked one young man who had just broken his neck in a skiing accident.
- "Can I have kids? Will they have MS too?" asked a young woman with multiple sclerosis.
- "How can I meet women now?" a stroke patient wanted to know.
- "Why don't I have feeling in my penis anymore?" another young man asked.

These were all obvious questions, but when we searched for answers they were hard to come by. True, there were plenty of books on the topic, but they tended to be technical and jargon-laden, and none of them were particularly helpful in answering sexual questions in practical, day-to-day terms. The idea for this book grew out of that void.

At the time, little was known about the sexual possibilities for people with severe physical disabilities. Since then, of course, a great deal of research has been done. And thanks to ongoing medical advances and such progressive programs as the independent living movement, today many people with spinal cord injuries are marrying, having children, and enjoying sex more than ever.

This is not to downplay the physical and psychological trauma that accompanies spinal cord injury. Such disabilities entail dramatic, usually painful, changes in people's lives. At times, the adjustment can seem overwhelming, and it often breeds a sense of hopelessness and perhaps depression. Nevertheless, life doesn't end after spinal cord injuries, and neither do a person's relationships and sexual life.

In the first months following a spinal cord injury, it's natural for people not to feel sexual or have much interest in sexual activity. Even later, some people may decide not to engage in an active sex life. The important point to understand is that you have a choice; you can decide to renew—or to begin—sexual activity or not. Either way, coming to terms with your sexuality is a necessary step toward making a healthy adjustment to an injury. It will have a direct bearing on how you feel about yourself, how you relate to others, and how you care for yourself.

This book is meant as a down-to-earth discussion of sexual questions for people with spinal cord injuries. The introduction discusses the anatomy of spinal cord injuries and of sexuality and also discusses the phases of sexual stimulation. Chapter 1 reviews some basic postinjury questions and rehabilitation issues. Chapter 2 introduces concerns about self-esteem, dating, relationships, sex, and marriage. Chapter 3 delves into the physical aspects of sex. Chapter 4 discusses fertility and parenting issues for both men and women and also questions about feminine hygiene. Chapter 5 reviews questions about the important topic of sexually transmitted diseases. Finally, the appendices provide a glossary and a list of independent living programs and other resources in the United States and Canada.

We have drawn on the insights and experiences of numerous people with spinal cord injuries. The book is written in a simple question-and-answer format, and we have tried to use language that is easily understood without being offensive. Our intention has been to inform, enlighten, and inspire, not make judgments about sexual habits, tastes, or orientations. We hope that doctors and rehabilitation professionals will also find it helpful.

A final word of caution: The questions addressed in this book don't always lend themselves to easy answers, and the answers will often prove to be different for different people. In other words, our responses are not necessarily meant as solutions, nor are they going to be appropriate for everybody. What we have tried to provide are both sound information and a basic framework that will allow you to begin answering the question for yourself. In doing so, we hope you will be better able to discover, or rediscover, the joys of your own sexuality in the aftermath of a spinal cord injury. In that spirit, this book is dedicated to you.

Acknowledgments

The idea of a handbook on sexuality for people with spinal cord injury began when a group of people in Boston were conducting Sexual Attitude Reassessment (SAR) workshops. The facilitators of these programs spent many hours talking about sexual issues, developing training programs, and working with other people on the sexual aspects of disability. Our appreciation goes to these friends and early SAR participants for their assistance in the formulation of this project. A special thanks goes to Jacqueline Ducharme, who also participated in these programs and has been an ongoing source of support.

As this book was developed, people with spinal cord injury and other disabilities provided their input, suggestions, and personal experiences. Much gratitude and thanks go to these people who made themselves available. The following individuals served as members of our consumer advisory board and contributed their personal experiences and knowledge to this book: Patrick Ryan, Paul Spooner, Cindy Percell, Thomas Bosco, Pam Kelly-Berkley, and John Falco.

Our gratitude is also expressed to the Education and Training Foundation of the Paralyzed Veterans of America for their financial support of this project. Their encouragement and support made our visions of this handbook become a reality.

SEXUALITY
After Spinal
Cord Injury

Introduction

Spinal cord injury is a medical condition, usually brought on by disease or accident, that has a severe effect on a number of body systems. These injuries usually result in paralysis of motor abilities such as walking, loss of sensation in certain parts of the body, and loss of bladder and bowel functioning. Although the symptoms may be temporary in some cases, they are often permanent. The motor and sensory changes may be either complete or incomplete, depending on the severity of the injury.

INTRODUCTION TO SPINAL CORD INJURY

Spinal cord injury most often occurs to young men between the ages of 15 and 29, but it can happen to men or women at any time throughout the life span. In the early 20th century, the life expectancy of a person with this type of injury was approximately 18 months following injury. Today, as a result of improved paramedical services and medical advances, the life expectancy for a person with a spinal cord injury is similar to that of a person without a disability.

In many ways, the medical prognosis for people with spinal cord injury varies from one person to the next. Motor and sensory impairments depend on the level of the spinal cord injury and the completeness or incompleteness of the tear (or lesion). For people with complete lesion of the spinal cord, there will be a total loss of sensation and motor ability

1

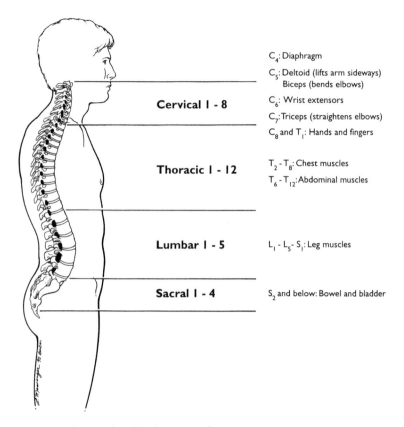

Figure 1.   The spinal cord and corresponding nerves.

below the level of injury. Injuries that occur to the neck region (called the cervical area) usually result in some paralysis to all four limbs; this level of injury is referred to as *quadriplegia*. Injuries occurring in the back (the thoracic, lumbar, or sacral areas) will result in some paralysis to the legs; this type of injury is referred to as *paraplegia*.

Motor Involvement

People with quadriplegia may have impaired breathing, especially if the lesion is at the C1, C2, or C3 level. For these individuals, the use of a ventilator is often necessary either for part or for all of the day. Movement may be limited to facial muscles. There is usually little movement below the head, except for people with injuries at C3 or below, who may have shoulder movement.

People with injuries at the C4 level will often be able to use their shoulders and biceps, which allows for some use of the arms and hands. Usually, fine motor skills are not possible for people with injuries at these levels. At the C6 level, there is often some use of the wrist, which may allow for independent transfers out of the wheelchair as well as the ability to feed oneself. At the C7 or C8 level, finger movements may be possible, although impaired.

A spinal cord injury in the thoracic, lumbar, or sacral area results in some paralysis of the lower extremities. An injury at the thoracic level often affects muscles of the chest, abdomen, and legs. As a result, people with these injuries typically have difficulties with balance and stability. People with injuries at this level require the use of a manual wheelchair and complete most functions with the upper parts of the body. Injuries in the lumbar area often affect the hip and leg functioning. Walking may be possible with long leg braces but often requires such strong endurance that a wheelchair is preferred, especially for longer distances. Sacral injuries affect leg functioning, although walking is definitely possible with short leg braces.

Sensory Involvement

Spinal cord injury often results in a loss of feeling below the level of injury. For people with an incomplete injury, this loss of sensation may be partial, depending on the severity of the lesions. These people may not be able to differentiate between hard or soft touch, and their perceptions of pain or pleasure may be very different from before their injury. Loss of sensation therefore has a profound impact on sexual functioning, touch, and pain. The most significant complication from a loss of sensation is the inability to determine when to shift one's weight in the wheelchair. As a result, pressure sores or decubitus ulcers often develop, and their prevention requires close attention. These sores are caused by poor circulation from sitting in the wheelchair and result in damaged skin and tissue. Treatment can be a long, difficult process that may require staying out of the wheelchair for weeks or months at a time. Prevention, rather than treatment, is always preferred.

Bladder and Bowel Involvement

Bladder and bowel functioning is often affected by a spinal cord injury. Because the nerve pathways to control these functions are interrupted, the individual is unaware of the need to empty the bladder or bowel. Voluntary control of bladder and bowel is usually lost in a complete injury, and some control may be lost when the injury is incomplete. While a recently injured person is in the rehabilitation hospital, the doctor and nurses provide assistance in bladder functioning with an indwelling catheter. As the person proceeds through the rehabilitation program, this indwelling catheter is often replaced by a program of intermittent catheterization. Intermittent catheterizations require that a tube be inserted into the bladder on a regular basis to drain the urine. This type of program is designed to help the bladder fill and empty as it did before the injury. It also ensures that urine does not back up into the kidneys and cause infection. Many men, after spinal cord injury, eventually use an external urine collection device such as a condom catheter. This system allows urine to drain from the bladder and to be collected in either the leg or bed bag, which can be emptied as needed. There has been much research in designing an external collection device for women, but to date no single system has gained widespread approval.

Bowel training is considered to be much less complicated than bladder training for most people. Once a program has been established in the rehabilitation hospital, it continues on the same schedule after discharge. Typically, the person learns to empty his or her bowel once per day or every other day. Medications or aids used for stimulation may be helpful on an initial basis and sometimes can be discontinued after a short period. A regular program of emptying the bowel prevents accidents, constipation, or impaction of the bowels. With proper diet and good health, socially difficult situations can be avoided and the individual can expect a high degree of regularity.

Other Medical Conditions

Other medical conditions, such as muscle spasms, pain, or autonomic dysreflexia, are also common after a spinal cord injury. Respiratory functioning and temperature regulation may be compromised in some cases. These medical changes are usually discussed during the rehabilitation program, and proper care and precautions are taught. Often the staff hold spinal cord injury classes to familiarize patients with possible medical problems. If these issues were not discussed during your rehabilitation program, it may be a good idea to schedule a meeting with your primary or rehabilitation doctor to better understand how your body has changed since the injury.

MALE SEXUAL ANATOMY

The male sexual organs consist of a complex combination of tubes, glans, valves, and muscles that work together to produce sperm, store it, and deliver it outside of the body. A man's most obvious sexual organ is his penis, which can be either in the limp (or flaccid) stage or in the erect stage. Although differences in size may be noted when flaccid, most penises tend to be about the same size when fully erect. The penis consists largely of three sponge-type cylinders that have a network of spaces inside of them. Two of these cylinders are called the *corpora cavernosa* and are responsible for erection. The arteries bring blood into the penis, and as the penis becomes erect the veins become blocked so that blood is unable to escape. The third cylinder is located on the underside of the penis and contains the urethra. This sponge-like chamber extends to the tip of the penis at an area called the glans penis. This portion of the penis is covered by the foreskin. Many men for religious and other reasons have had the foreskin removed during a surgical procedure called a circumcision. This is usually done soon after birth, but in some cases it is done later in life.

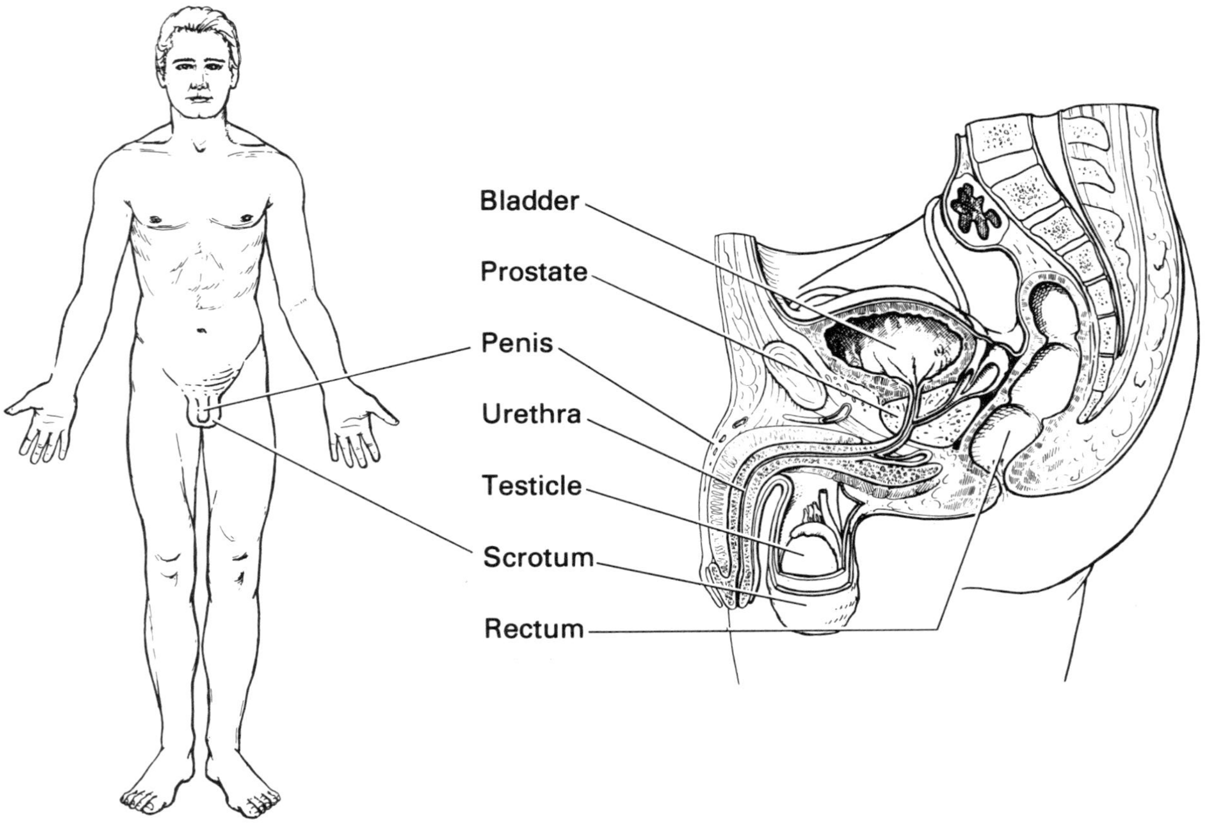

Figure 2. The male sexual anatomy.

Bladder
Prostate
Penis
Urethra
Testicle
Scrotum
Rectum

The urethra, the small tube that runs the length of the penis, empties urine from the body and is a passageway for the ejaculation of semen, which contains the sperm. Usually, when the man is about to ejaculate, there is a valve that shuts off the bladder so that urine and sperm cannot be mixed together. For men with spinal cord injury, this mechanism may work differently, as the semen sometimes goes back into the bladder rather than being ejaculated out of the body; when the man urinates later, the semen will leave the body with the urine. This process is called *retrograde ejaculation.*

Hanging down below the penis is a loose sack of skin called the scrotum. The scrotum is divided into two parts, and each one of these parts contains a testicle. There are many different kinds of muscles in the scrotum that work to raise and lower the testicles depending on the temperature outside the body. This process helps the testicles to produce sperm, which is also stored in the testicles. Although both testicles are generally the same size, many men notice that one of the testicles will hang down lower than the other. Sperm are continually produced in the testicles from the time that a boy reaches puberty. The sperm, once they have been produced, pass through a series of tubes until they reach a portion of the penis called the vas deferens. This is the main tube of the male sexual system, and it leads from the testicles into the urethra.

The prostate gland is another important part of this system and works to help deliver the sperm outside of the body. The prostate manufactures the white, milky substance that carries the sperm. When the man becomes sexually excited, the muscles of the prostate and other muscles begin to contract and push the semen down the urethra until it ejaculates out the end of the penis.

MEN'S SEXUAL HEALTH

Good sexual health for men involves maintaining the cleanliness of the sexual organs and conducting regular self-examinations of the penis and scrotum. Although self-examinations are common among women, they are equally important for men. Regular checking of the penis and scrotum can help ensure that infections are caught and treated early. Self-examinations can also help detect cancer of the penis or testicles. At least once a month a man should examine his sexual organs, comparing the testicles and checking for lumps, masses, or any significant changes in the texture of the skin. Any lumps or thickened area should then be checked by a physician.

The best time for a self-examination is after a warm shower or bath, when the muscles are relaxed. Gently touch the entire area of the penis and scrotum, noting any pain, bumps, or lumps. Notice any changes in skin textures as well on either the front or back side of the testicles, and note any signs of redness or other indications of infection. If there is a foreskin, pull it back to notice signs of discharge or other irregularities. Be especially watchful of signs of skin break-downs in both the penis and scrotum, as the warm, moist environment of this area can promote the growth of bacteria and infection. Although most physicians can be helpful in problems of this nature, a urologist is a specialist in the urinary tract.

FEMALE SEXUAL ANATOMY

The entire external genitalia of a woman is called the vulva. This includes the vagina, labia, and clitoris. The vagina is a soft tube that is several inches long and can be extended during sexual intercourse. The outer end of the vagina is extremely sensitive and excitable. Its inner lining is soft and moist and produces a slippery fluid during sexual excitement. This fluid allows a man's penis to enter and helps during sexual intercourse. The external area directly above the vagina is called the mons veneris. This area, usually covered by pubic hair, is made of fatty tissue and offers protection to the external labia and clitoris. The mons also tends to provide a cushion for some positions during intercourse, such as when the woman is sitting up. The labia minora and majora are folds of skin that surround the vaginal opening.

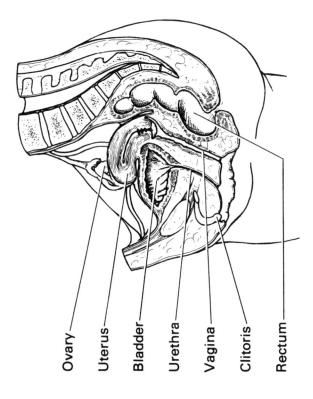

Ovary

Uterus

Bladder

Urethra

Vagina

Clitoris

Rectum

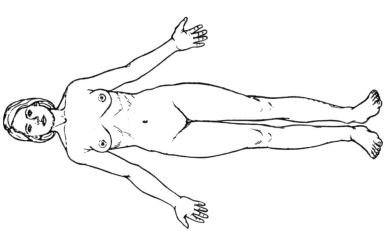

Figure 3.   The female sexual anatomy.

These contain numerous blood vessels and various glands that produce oils and secretions.

The clitoris is much like the male penis and contains very sensitive nerves similar to the head of the penis. It also fills with blood and becomes erect when the woman becomes sexually excited. For many women, stimulation of this area brings on climax. The tip of the clitoris is covered by a small area of tissues usually referred to as the clitoris hood. The hood protects the sensitive nerves located in the clitoris. The size and shape of the hood varies among women and is not related to the amount of sexual pleasure that a woman can receive. The hood can also be a source of infection and must be kept clean at all times.

The primary reproductive organs of the woman are the two ovaries that lie on the inside of the lower part of the abdomen. The ovaries are responsible for storing the ova or eggs until the girl reaches puberty. After puberty, the ova begin to mature, usually one per month about halfway between the woman's menstrual cycle. When the egg reaches maturity and is released, it is transported, along with its fluid, into the opening at the end of the fallopian tube. It then moves down the fallopian tube toward the uterus. At the neck of the uterus is an opening to the vagina called the cervix. This small opening allows thousands of sperm to enter the uterus during sexual intercourse.

WOMEN'S SEXUAL HEALTH

Because a woman's genitals are not as visible as the man's penis, many women are unfamiliar with the structure, shape, and appearance of their genital area. Self-examinations allow each woman to recognize what is "normal" for her and thus to recognize problems at an early stage and ask relevant medical questions if a physician's visit becomes necessary. For women, self-examinations should consist of both a vaginal self-examination and a breast examination.

Undertaking a self-examination of the vagina requires some background reading and some basic instructions from friends or health professionals. Relevant reading materials can usually be obtained from women's health clinics, hospital clinics, physicians' offices, and some pharmacies. In order to do a self-examination, a woman will need to obtain a speculum, an instrument that will open the walls of the vagina so that she can look inside. Disposable plastic speculums can be obtained in a medical supply store, pharmacy, or doctor's office. Other needed supplies include a mirror, flashlight, pillows, and a water-soluble jelly. Some women like to have a pad and pencil handy in case they want to write down a note for future questions. Before beginning, it is important to wash hands thoroughly and to empty the bladder.

To examine the vulva, position the mirror so that the vagina and labia can be viewed. Note the color, size, and shape of the clitoris, the labia, and the opening of the vagina. Also, note any secretions from the vagina. Vaginal secretions of certain types are normal and will vary according to the phase of the menstrual cycle. For an internal examination, being able to relax and finding the correct position are critical. Also, having some practice with the speculum will help the examination to go smoothly.

Breast self-examinations are painless and simple and generally take only a few moments. The best time to do this examination is usually a day or two after your menstrual period, when the tenderness and fullness have subsided. It is a good idea to examine yourself at the same time each month so that the breast tissue is consistent from one exam to the next. In front of a mirror, check the size and contour of each breast. Gently squeeze each nipple to check for any unusual discharge. Feel the breast for unusual lumps or thickness, using the three middle fingers of one hand to palpate the breast in a circular motion. Specific directions for conducting a breast and vaginal examination should be obtained from a women's health clinic or doctor's office.

THE PHASES OF SEXUAL AROUSAL

Masters and Johnson (1966) were researchers who spent their careers conducting scientific studies on sex and the physical changes that occur as a result of sexual stimulation. Their work provided us with new information on sexual functioning and opened the door to better understanding of human sexuality. One of the most important aspects of their research was the discovery that the entire body undergoes changes during sexual excitement. Before their work, people generally believed that the genitals were the only organs of the body directly affected by sexual excitement. To explain the changes that occur in the body, Masters and Johnson divided the sexual act into four distinct phases.

Men and women go through these phases in ways that are both similar and different. All people react similarly to sexual excitement, but individual needs and the timing of reactions may be very different. Therefore, the needs of men and women do not always occur at the same time, and frustration can easily occur as one individual reaches satisfaction before his or her partner. Becoming a sensual and sexual partner requires, to some extent, knowledge about the changes that occur for both men and women as they become sexually excited.

Phase One: Excitement

All people go through a period of time in which sexual excitement begins to build. This can occur gradually or quickly depending on the individual person and the intensity of the situation. As stimulation increases and the penis and vulva are touched and fondled, couples will notice a stronger desire for sexual release. Watching a partner become aroused and using sexual language while becoming aroused generally increases the level of excitement for most people.

Knowledge about the arousal process is not well understood, although scientists do know that hormones play an important part, as do certain portions of the brain. As an individual becomes aroused, increases in blood pressure, heart rate, and breathing follow. Also, the nipples of both men and women may become erect. As the excitement builds, a man's penis may begin to become hard and a woman's vagina may begin to moisten. The hardening of the penis or moistening of the vagina may not occur in many people with spinal cord injuries, but this depends on the severity and level of the injury. Other signs of sexual arousal usually remain the same for individuals with a spinal cord injury.

Phase Two: Plateau

The plateau phase is a continuation of the excitement phase, with all bodily changes increasing in intensity. Both men and women will note ongoing increases in breathing, blood pressure or flushness, and heart rate. Nipples continue to become erect, and both penis and vagina reach their full state of excitement. A man's penis is generally sufficiently hard for penetration, and a woman's vagina expands and becomes sufficiently lubricated for insertion of the penis, if intercourse is desired. If the penis and vagina have not responded completely, erectile aids and artificial lubricants may be used to complete the process. As sexual desire increases, both men's and women's genitals tend to increase in size with muscular tensions and spasms. The body becomes increasingly sensitive to touch, and the urge for stimulation of the genitals becomes overpowering. For men, pre-ejaculation is often secreted from the penis in varying amounts.

During this phase of sexual excitement, partners use verbal and nonverbal communication to signal readiness for intercourse or further oral or manual stimulation. Visual, auditory, and tactile sensations can increase the intensity of this phase. There is often a sense of pending climax.

Phase Three: Orgasm

As the level of sexual excitement increases, the partners may reach a point in which their climax is inevitable. Their climax may not occur simultaneously, however, and communication, sensitivity, and attention to the partner's needs may be especially critical at this time. Men generally are able to achieve one climax and ejaculation during each sexual experience, while women are capable of multiple orgasms depending on both physical and psychological factors. There is a sense of urgency during this phase: Bodily changes continue to increase, and during intercourse the man's thrusting becomes more rapid and deep and the man's penis and the woman's vagina experience ongoing rhythmic contractions. Some men report the ability to achieve an orgasm at this time without having an erection. Memories, fantasies, and a sense of closeness may add to the physical pleasures of ejaculation and orgasm and can enhance the orgasm experience for both men and women.

The intensity of these bodily sensations again depends on the condition of the spinal cord and the age of the individual. People with spinal cord injuries may not experience the intense physical genital sensation they may have before their injury, but they often report being flooded with other pleasurable sensations both physical and psychological. Experience with love making and awareness of one's bodily reaction usually increase the pleasurable sensations over time since injury. Men and women who are older tend to have less intense orgasms, although often equally enjoyable because of their familiarity with each other and their comfort with their own sexuality. The sensation of orgasm is often different for men and women. For men, there is usually a single, strong release, while women enjoy either single or multiple peaks and a widespread feeling of sensuality throughout the body.

Phase Four: Resolution

Following climax, a couple enters the resolution phase, which signals return to the presexual state. The rate of return for men and women can be very different. It is not uncommon for a man to enter this phase while the woman may still be moving toward orgasm. Consideration for each other is an important psychological aspect of this phase. Typically, men lose their erections immediately after ejaculation and release, whereas women may return much more slowly. There is a gradual decline in swelling of the breast, labia, and vagina at this time. Emotionally, this can be a time of closeness, sharing, and intimacy that further enhances the love-making experience if the couple share strong feelings for one another.

During this resolution phase, men are generally unable to regain an erection and thus experience a refractory period.

The length of time for this period can range from about 10 minutes in younger men to several hours for older men. Women do not experience a refractory period and are capable of further sexual excitement during this time, as they experience a much more gradual return to the presexual state. If a man uses various aids, such as injections or a vacuum device, to assist him in achieving an erection, he may not experience a refractory period, as his penis will stay hard regardless of orgasm.

The resolution phase of sexual activity is generally a time in which the couple may feel close, share their feelings for one another, and enjoy the special intimacy of being together. If both members of the relationship have enjoyed the experience, regardless of orgasm, this can be a special time of sharing and tenderness.

REFERENCE

Masters, W.H., & Johnson, V.E. (1966). *Human sexual response.* Boston: Little, Brown.

1

Rehabilitation and Community Integration

1. Do all people get depressed after a spinal cord injury?

2. Will I ever get over my anger and sadness?

3. Is it normal to worry so much about rejection after spinal cord injury?

4. As time passes, will my sexual functioning get back to where it was before I got hurt?

5. How long after my injury should I wait before sex?

6. Is it okay to be sexual in the rehabilitation center?

7. Is my nurse or therapist allowed to be intimate with me?

8. Whom do I ask questions about sex?

9. My doctor gets embarrassed easily. How should I help him?

10. Should I see a sex therapist?

11. What is a urologist, and what does he do?

12. Will my insurance pay for me to see a urologist or sex therapist?

13. How do I find a gynecologist?

14. What is a sexual surrogate?

15. What services are available from independent living programs?

16. Whom do I talk to about sex after I leave the rehabilitation center?

17. Is it okay to have sex with my personal care attendant (PCA)?

18. My partner often feels like my nurse. Is that normal?

1 Do all people get depressed after a spinal cord injury?

In the past, mental health professionals felt that all people went through various stages in the adjustment to their spinal cord injury. These included periods of denial, depression, anger, and eventually acceptance. Today, this theory has been discarded. It is believed that all people go through their own individual process that may or may not include depression.

A reaction to a disability is an individual process that contains personal feelings and thoughts. If you do find yourself depressed after your injury, this should improve with time, especially if you are able to share your feelings with another person. Many people have found peer counseling is helpful after injury. Talking about your feelings will help give you a sense of mastery and control. It can also help you to develop healthy ways to handle the stress and pressure that you may be experiencing. If the depression does not improve within a few months after your injury, you may want to consider getting some counseling.

2 Will I ever get over my anger and sadness?

Feelings of anger and sadness are normal after trauma such as a spinal cord injury. These feelings are a natural reaction to the sudden changes that you may now be experiencing. Mental health professionals refer to this as part of the grieving process; how long these feelings last and how intense they will be vary for each person. Women may have an advantage over men in this regard, as women are much more sanctioned by society to express their feelings and discuss emotionally painful topics. Many people will try to offer reassurance and tell you that your reactions are unnecessary. It is best if you can find a person to talk with who will listen, offer positive suggestions, and provide emotional support, no matter how sad or angry you feel.

Some people find that a mental health or peer counselor can be helpful. They may be able to offer suggestions that will assist you in the difficult adjustments you are experiencing. For some people, medications can also be helpful if the sadness is severe and interfering with daily activities. There is no shame in seeking assistance with feelings that cause distress and pain. Certainly, if you are having suicidal feelings and thoughts, it would be wise to speak with a professional and get assistance.

3 Is it normal to worry so much about rejection after spinal cord injury?

Most men and women worry a great deal about rejection for a period of time after their spinal cord injury. It is not unusual for this fear to be present during the first sexual experiences after an injury or for these fears to get even worse after a couple has been intimate. These worries may be a result of feelings of inadequacy. Some people also worry that their partner may be unfaithful and have an affair. There is often a concern that sex will not be satisfying to either of them. These concerns must be discussed so that both partners have the opportunity to talk about the changes that have occurred in the relationship. If these concerns are not discussed, there is a greater chance that the spinal cord injury will create a barrier between the couple.

4 As time passes, will my sexual functioning get back to where it was before I got hurt?

Because sexual, bladder, and bowel functioning are controlled in the very lowest portions of the spinal cord (S2–S4), these bodily functions are usually impaired in people who have spinal cord injuries. Although there may be improvements over time, some residual difficulties always remain. Improvements tend to occur slowly during the first year after injury. After that, any additional changes and return of functioning will be even more gradual and the chances of return more remote as time passes. You may notice some gradual changes in the quality of your orgasms, lubrications, and engorgement of nipples, vulva, or penis. If your sexual functioning was changed because of the injury, however, there is probably a good possibility it will not totally return to what it was before. Try to enjoy your sexuality for what it is today, rather than waiting and hoping that it will change.

5 How long after my injury should I wait before sex?

There are no absolutes to this question. Some people wait years before becoming sexually active; others want to explore their sexual response immediately. Some people experiment sexually before they leave the rehabilitation hospital with staff members, spouses, or friends; others masturbate. When you become sexually active is your decision and depends on a number of factors, including your health, emotions, age, relationship status, level of injury, and social values. Listen to your body, your feelings, and your sexual desires.

6 Is it okay to be sexual in the rehabilitation center?

Exploring your body and enjoying sexual pleasures is a natural part of life that you can certainly enjoy even in the rehabilitation center. During rehabilitation, it is a good idea to touch yourself, explore your body, and get as much information as you can. For example, don't hesitate to ask your nurse whether you become erect when you receive a catheterization. This is important information, especially if you are unable to see your penis or if the sensation is decreased.

A word of caution, however. Although sexual experimentation during rehabilitation may be a good idea, doing it in the privacy of your room is also important. In addition, don't expect staff members to be sexual with you or pressure them into embarrassing situations. Touching staff members in a sexual way is inappropriate and is considered sexual harassment. Respect the people working with you, and keep your intimate relationships separate from the ones you develop with staff members.

7 Is my nurse or therapist allowed to be intimate with me?

Your health care providers are not allowed to be intimate with you while you are in the hospital. If they do become sexually involved with you, their jobs may be in danger; also, it may be very difficult for them to handle the strong emotions associated with the relationship. After discharge, each hospital has its own rules, but generally it is considered to be a personal and private matter. The tendency to develop strong romantic and sexual feelings toward people who are taking care of you is quite normal and common. This is a person with whom you feel safe and who is familiar with spinal cord injury. It is a professional relationship, however, and to change it into a romantic relationship most often is difficult and destructive to one or both of you. Be very careful with the feelings that develop between you and the people providing services to you. The balance of power is always unequal, and your needs are very different.

8   Whom do I ask questions about sex?

While in the hospital, you should feel comfortable asking questions of almost any member of your rehabilitation team. If your therapist, nurse, or doctor doesn't have the answer, he or she should be able to point you in the right direction, to either a professional or peer counselor. In addition, most rehabilitation facilities have printed information about sexuality when you feel ready to learn more about the subject. Inquire about classes on sexuality. Your program may have education videos that are available to people while in the hospital.

After you leave the hospital, it may be more difficult to find answers to your questions. Generally, independent living centers have resources available or peer counselors. Talking with someone who has a disability can be very helpful. Other people may have worked out solutions to particular problems or can give you firsthand information on what to expect. Another source of information may be printed materials, like this book, that are geared for you. Generally, these publications provide the names of professionals who work in this area, as well as organizations that are dedicated to this topic. Most important, don't stop looking until you feel satisfied that you have received the information you were looking for.

My doctor gets embarrassed easily. How should I help him?

It is not your responsibility to educate your doctor or to help him or her feel more comfortable with sexual questions. The solution is to find another doctor who can speak with you honestly and answer your questions openly. It is the doctor's responsibility to learn about the topic and deal with it without embarrassment. If your doctor is unable to do this, he or she should refer you to someone who can. If the doctor is unable or unwilling to refer you to someone else, take the situation into your own hands and find yourself a new doctor who meets your needs.

10 Should I see a sex therapist?

People with spinal cord injuries usually don't need to see a sex therapist to enjoy a healthy and satisfying sexual life. If you want education and information about your sexual possibilities, you can ask your psychologist, physician, rehabilitation therapist, or peer counselor. If you have had difficulties with sex in the past, however, seeing a sex therapist may be a good idea. For example, if you have questions about your sexual identity (heterosexual or homosexual), if you have been sexually abused, or if you have had problems with, say, erection before your injury, seeing a sex therapist may be helpful and supportive. Generally, though, you are adapting to a new situation, and patience, practice, and communication will be all that you need.

11 What is a urologist, and what does he do?

Urologists are physicians trained to diagnose and treat disorders of the genital/urinary tract. They typically perform tests to determine the effectiveness of your bladder management program and will advise your rehabilitation doctors as to the status of your bladder. They are also experts on male fertility and impotence. You should consider contacting a urologist if you are a man with a spinal cord injury and you are interested in having a child or if you are having difficulties with your erections. It is a good idea to have a urologist who is familiar with your bladder program, should you later develop urinary tract infections or stones.

12 Will my insurance pay for me to see a urologist or sex therapist?

This is a difficult question because regulations vary from state to state and are constantly being reconsidered. Because erection problems in men with spinal cord injury have a physical cause, a urology visit is covered by most private insurance. If you receive Social Security, you probably also have Medical Part A and Part B benefits. Part A pays for inpatient services, and Part B pays for a portion of outpatient services. It is necessary for your doctor to provide your insurance company with an acceptable diagnosis category demonstrating that treatment is medically necessary.

Sex therapists are covered under the mental health benefits of most private insurance and Part B of Medicare. Usually, a portion of their hourly fee is paid if the therapist has the correct license and is a provider for your particular insurance company. In most states, there is a $500 ceiling for mental health services per calendar year. The following two steps are recommended:

1. Call your doctor to determine whether he or she is a member of your insurance company's network. Find out what tests will be needed and whether they are covered by Medicare or your insurance. Determine the doctor's policy regarding copayments, fee schedule, missed appointments, and other financial matters. Be an informed consumer, and remember that you are purchasing a service. You have rights that must be respected by your doctors.

2. Call your insurance company or Medicare prior to your first visit to determine eligibility. Also find out whether approval is necessary prior to your first visit.

13 How do I find a gynecologist?

Finding a gynecologist who is sensitive to the needs of a woman with a disability can be a frustrating and difficult task. Your primary care physician or rehabilitation doctor may be helpful in this regard. He or she may have suggestions and know gynecologists with experience in this area. Other women with disabilities, however, are probably your best source of information and can tell you whom they would recommend or avoid. Also, call your local independent living center for information, or check with the National Spinal Cord Foundation for a referral in your area. It may be necessary to try several doctors before you find one who meets your needs and feels comfortable to you. Don't be afraid to switch doctors until you find the right person who has experience with disability and is sensitive. You have a right to good gynecological care and should not settle for anything less than the best. If you have a managed care insurance, don't forget to get a referral from your primary care doctor.

14 What is a sexual surrogate?

A sexual surrogate is a type of therapist who helps people with sexual difficulties through physical and sexual contact. Sexual surrogates believe that a person can gain confidence by achieving positive experiences and successes by direct sexual contact. They believe that, after people gain confidence in their sexual behavior, they will overcome problems in sexual performance and feel more comfortable with other partners.

Although sexual surrogates were somewhat popular back in the 1970s, there are very few such programs today. Sexual surrogates have run into legal and ethical problems, which have intensified as helping professions become more regulated. In addition, the spread of sexually transmitted diseases discouraged many people from seeking this type of direct treatment. Surrogates were often confused with prostitutes, and a dependency sometimes developed by individuals fearful of establishing an intimate relationship with a partner.

15 What services are available from independent living programs?

Independent living programs offer a broad range of services that can be of great assistance in helping you lead the most independent life possible. Advocacy services, personal care assistance, housing, and educational programs are often offered, as is peer counseling in sexuality, accessibility, housing, employment, and psychological adjustment. These programs also provide important social opportunities and information about a broad range of community agencies and services. It's a good idea to connect with a program after you leave the rehabilitation center and find out how it can be helpful to you.

16 Whom do I talk to about sex after I leave the rehabilitation center?

Ideally, sexual advice should come from someone who is knowledgeable, trustworthy, nonjudgmental, and open. You may be able to find a health care or mental health professional with whom you feel comfortable and to whom you can ask important questions about sex.

Peers are another good source for sexual information. Friends, especially those who share your values and experiences, may be willing to hear your concerns and talk about sexual issues. Don't be afraid to ask.

You may also wish to speak with someone with a similar injury about its effect on his or her sexual life. Talking with such a person—a process called peer counseling—is a great way to get information on any issue related to your injury. In fact, many people feel that talking with a peer is the best way to overcome problems and get support. Perhaps only a person who has been through a similar situation can know what you are facing and understand the difficulties in finding a solution. Most people with spinal cord injuries are nervous about peer counseling at first, but have found it to be a very valuable experience. You can locate a peer counselor through your local independent living center or by contacting a community agency that provides services to people with disabilities.

If you are in a relationship, it is especially important to discuss your sexual concerns, likes, dislikes, needs, and feelings with your partner. This openness will bring closeness and understanding to your relationship.

17 Is it okay to have sex with my personal care attendant (PCA)?

The answer to this question is a strong *no*. The PCA is there to deliver caregiving services, and you're there as the consumer of those services. Your needs come first; the PCA is supposed to put his or her personal needs aside.

Personal relationships are supposed to be reciprocal, with all parties having their needs met. Start mixing business and relationships and it can be trouble. What if you have a fight and the PCA needs space—and doesn't show up for work? Your health and safety depend on the PCA being responsible, but switching back into business roles is easier said than done. What if you are angry at the PCA and refuse care?

Occasionally, individuals become involved with their assistants, but you and your PCA would need to be exceptionally mature to sustain a personal relationship. It is generally not a good idea and can lead to many complications.

18 My partner often feels like my nurse. Is that normal?

It is very common for a spouse or partner to feel like a nurse if he or she is one of the primary people involved in the physical care of the person with a spinal cord injury. One of the most common problems in relationships is confusion regarding the roles that each member of a relationship plays as a lover, a friend, or a care provider. Once the person takes on more than one of these roles, confusion can ensue and the relationship can develop difficulties and create resentment.

Whenever possible, try not to let your partner provide most of your physical care. If possible, use the services of a home health aide or a personal attendant for bowel care or to change dressings. If your partner must provide medical care for you, try to have it done when sexual contact is not feasible. In other words, separate the two roles as much as you can. Do your best to listen and support each other in an open, nondefensive manner.

2

Emotional and Social Concerns

1. What is body image?

2. How do I keep my confidence when I have to ask others for everything?

3. How do I improve my appearance?

4. Can I still wear a dress in a wheelchair?

5. How am I going to try on clothes in a store?

6. I don't like my body. How will other people react?

7. How could anyone ever be interested in me?

8. Why do people treat me like a sibling?

9. People only see the wheelchair. How can I get them to see me?

10. Won't people think I'm desperate if I'm assertive?

11. How do I meet potential partners?

12. I am gay/lesbian. How do I meet potential partners?

13. How concerned should I be about accessibility to social meeting places?

14. How do I tell someone that I am interested in him/her?

15. Should I date another person with a disability?

16. Are there special things to think about before getting involved in a relationship?

17. When should I tell a new partner about my injury?

18. Will someone want to stay with me in a long-term relationship?

19. How do I know if I am in love?

20. Can I still have a sex life?

21. How often should I want to have sex?

22. I've never had sex. What will it be like?

23. Why am I not interested in sex anymore?

24. Is it normal to worry about sex so much?

25. I feel so passive now. How can I really be sexual?

26. How can I feel like a man again?

27. How can I feel more sexy?

28. Will I develop sexually like my friends?

29. How do I tell my parents about my sexual activity?

30. Can someone become a homosexual as a result of an injury?

31. How do I know if I am a homosexual?

32. What is it like to be gay or lesbian and have a spinal cord injury?

33. How does a person communicate about sex?

34. How important is sex in a relationship?

35. Will my partner still be turned on?

36. I want to have sex, but my partner has lost interest. What should I do?

37. How do I say no to my partner?

38. Is there anything I can do to make sex better?

39. Will his penis fall out of my vagina during intercourse?

40. Will my vagina be tight enough for my partner to enjoy intercourse?

41. I have not engaged in sex for years. Can I be sexually active now?

42. What should I do if my partner becomes abusive?

43. Can a man be sexually abused?

44. Should I go to a prostitute?

45. Can I ever get married?

46. How soon should you get married after a spinal cord injury?

47. Do marriages last after a spinal cord injury? My spouse feels like my nurse. Is that normal?

48. When should people see a marriage counselor?

49. How will my sex life change as I get older?

50. Is there such a thing as male menopause?

51. Is it true that women stop having sex after menopause?

52. Will I need hormone replacement therapy when I go through menopause?

1 What is body image?

Body image is something that you hear about often when you have a spinal cord injury. It is a psychological term that refers to how you see and feel about your own body. After a traumatic injury, our feelings about our bodies are in a state of change. It may take some time before you feel good about how you look. Some people find it difficult to look in the mirror after their injury and don't like what they see. It is natural to go through a period when you feel unsure about yourself. If you have a negative view of yourself, give some thought to how you might improve your looks. Sometimes little changes can make a big difference. Look at your clothes, your hair, your facial expressions, and your posture. Can they be changed or improved? What would happen if you joined a gym and began an exercise program? Think about ways to feel better about yourself.

2 How do I keep my confidence when I have to ask others for everything?

Requesting help need not be damaging to your confidence and self-esteem. We are taught to be independent from an early age, and requesting assistance often goes against that training. But remember you still have a choice to ask for help when you need it and refuse it when it may be unnecessary; keeping this sense of control is critical. Your attitude toward assistance will also affect your self-confidence over the long run. Some people already know how to offer assistance in a way that preserves your dignity and self-respect; others may need to be taught to assist you in a way that keeps you in control and feeling good about yourself. You will need to be clear, firm, polite, and assertive in giving instructions to other people. It takes time to feel comfortable asking for help. Start with people you trust, if possible, and get their feedback regarding your instructions and your attitude.

3 How do I improve my appearance?

The first step in feeling better about your appearance is to explore your own attitudes regarding disability. Society's values and view of beauty have often been ingrained in us since childhood, but these views can be destructive. For example, why is it not socially acceptable to use a catheter instead of a toilet or to use a wheelchair as a way of moving around? The wheelchair may feel limiting, but it also provides independence and freedom, valuable commodities to each one of us. Freeing ourselves from societal views regarding attractiveness and disability may take time, but the result is well worth the effort. Be patient.

A second step in improving our sense of attractiveness is to focus on strengths, instead of weaknesses. This sounds easy, but can be very difficult. It's hard not to be preoccupied with the parts of ourselves that we feel bad about. Often, feelings of shame have existed for years and have nothing to do with disability, but a disability can bring negative feelings to the surface. Make a realistic appraisal of your attractive features, and keep reminding yourself of them. If necessary, leave notes around the house or on the mirror to remind yourself of your positive features.

Another important step is to stop comparing yourself with others. Instead, be realistic with yourself and see what needs more work and what you already feel good about. It also makes sense to seek support from family and friends to assist you in this process, but find people who are empathic rather than sympathetic. An empathic person is a good listener, who is not trying to build you up with false praise and who can hear your feelings, both positive and negative; a merely sympathetic listener tends to feel sorry for you and treat you as an inferior.

In addition, learn to receive honest feedback from others and especially to receive their compliments. Don't make explanations or contradict the compliment. Start by saying "Thank you," even if you don't feel comfortable receiving the praise. Little by little, you'll be able to say it and mean it.

One other suggested technique to improve your sense of attractiveness is to create a "spa" experience in the bath or shower, using all your senses to explore your body in a healthy way. Feel the touch of the water, the temperature and texture of the cloth or sponge. Notice the sounds and taste the water; feel the slipperiness of the soap, and the feel of yourself as you explore various parts of your body. As you touch and explore, appreciate your body and its beauty, so that you leave your bath with a sense of relaxation and openness. This simple experience can help you reconnect with feelings of attractiveness and sensuality.

Can I still wear a dress in a wheelchair?

You can wear anything that pleases you. There may be some styles that are not practical for sitting in a wheelchair, but the range of options is still very wide. Check with an occupational therapist or other women you may know through your local independent living center. Some companies make dresses and other clothing especially for people who use a wheelchair. This clothing is typically bought through catalogues and fits the special needs of a person using a wheelchair; for example, the clothing may have special fasteners and be specially designed for women using catheters. Don't be afraid of showing your legs and other parts of your body, even if you feel that they look different from before your injury.

5 How am I going to try on clothes in a store?

You generally have the choice of either trying on clothes in the store or at home. For a variety of reasons, you may not have the luxury of bringing them back and forth to try them on at home, and it may be easier to try them on in the store. Inquire about the dressing rooms, or check them out yourself to see if they are wheelchair accessible. If they are not accessible and you shop there often, think about writing a letter or speaking with the manager about the problem. In either case, the salesperson may have another suggestion about where you can try clothes on, perhaps in a staff room or a larger changing room somewhere else in the store. Asking for assistance may be difficult, especially at first, and it may make you feel embarrassed. But asking for assistance should not make you feel helpless. Find a friend or a salesperson who knows how to offer help without making you feel uncomfortable. Some people may be overly helpful, while others can be rude. Find or instruct someone how to give you help while at the same time preserving your dignity and self-respect.

6 I don't like my body. How will other people react?

The first step in feeling comfortable with others is to feel comfortable with your own body. How you value yourself is communicated nonverbally to others; your body language lets others know how you feel and causes them to respond to you in a similar fashion. Once you've been able to accept yourself, change what you can change, if it serves the best interest of your health and fitness. Otherwise, appreciate your body just the way it is. If you feel beautiful, people can sense that and will treat you as a person of beauty. Another way to empower yourself is to rehearse with a friend how you present yourself in social situations and how you explain to potential partners what to expect about how your body looks and works. This kind of rehearsal has also been useful in teaching people to be assertive in meeting others in medical, social, or work situations.

7 How could anyone ever be interested in me?

The idea that you are not good enough or don't deserve to be in a relationship is both very common and very destructive. Without learning to value themselves and developing a healthy self-respect, women in particular are in danger of attracting abusive men. It is important to realize that every person has assets and liabilities, and everyone is lovable. Disability does not change this. There is no reason to believe that you are unattractive or have nothing to offer in a relationship because of your injury. Talking with other people with similar injuries or joining a support group may help. Although these lessons may be difficult to learn, it is possible to like yourself again and to realize the potential you have to give and receive love.

8 Why do people treat me like a sibling?

If other people generally don't regard you as a sexual person, it may be because you do not perceive yourself in this light. Maybe you feel that you have lost your sexuality as a result of your injury or that others will no longer be interested in you. If the people you encounter are overlooking your sexuality, give some thought as to how you might enhance this perception of your self. Are there changes that you can make with your clothing, your appearance, or the way you relate to others? Is it possible for you to become more assertive in your decisions and to avoid the passive stance that others may see? In summary, others will see you in a sexual light only when you demonstrate that you have much to offer in an intimate relationship.

 People only see the wheelchair. How can I get them to see me?

You may be right. Some people will only see the wheelchair. But many others will look beyond the chair and see you as well. If you believe in yourself, you can convey your attractiveness by how you present yourself to other people. It is important to be friendly. Start conversations, and let other people get to know you. Dress attractively and express your own personal style through your clothes, hair, and general appearance. Get involved in life and share your interests with others. Let others see you as a person worth knowing, someone who has much to offer in a relationship. This level of comfort with yourself takes time and practice. There will be instances when you will feel frustrated and experience disappointments in trying to meet people. It's okay to feel bad for awhile, but it's also important to keep trying. Get support from friends and family as you start dating, and share the good and bad with people close to you.

10 Won't people think I'm desperate if I'm assertive?

Being assertive means being neither too passive nor too aggressive. If your partner finds it unacceptable for you to make suggestions, initiate sexual activity, or say what you want, watch out. That person has a need to control you, and you may have to address some of his or her own insecurities. If you find yourself being overly aggressive in a relationship, try to step back and think about what might be going on. Sometimes, being aggressive is a mask for feelings of anger, frustration, and lack of control. A relationship requires both partners to be mature and comfortable with each other. If you are being yourself and sensitive to the other person, you do not need to be responsible for that person's reaction to you.

11 How do I meet potential partners?

How did you meet people before your injury? Chances are you ran into them on every avenue of your life—at work, at restaurants and bars, at supermarkets and bus stops, you name it. In fact, the only place you didn't meet dates was sitting at home. The same is true now.

The first thing you have to do, then, is to get back into circulation. Begin staking out friendly turf with your family and friends. Talk with them about your injury and your fears about meeting people again.

Once you're out in public again, get into the habit of striking up conversations with strangers. One advantage for men of being in a wheelchair is that women who don't know you won't view you as a physical menace. Both men and women might also consider taking out a personal ad, joining a dating service, or volunteering for blind dates. Of course, you run pretty much the same risks—and you face the same long odds—playing these versions of the dating game as you did before your injury; but if you're up to it, why not give it a try?

Whatever you do, get comfortable talking about yourself and your injury. People will have a natural curiosity about how you got injured and how you are making do now. Kids are especially likely to ask you about how you got hurt, how your wheelchair works, can you do wheelies, and so on. So be prepared to discuss it all in an open, friendly way. Remember, there's always a chance that the child's parent will be nearby, and that parent may be either single or divorced. The fastest way to a parent's heart is through kindness and affection with his or her children. And a sure way to stay there is to treat him or her with the same consideration.

Of course, it may be more difficult to meet people because wheelchair accessibility limits the number of places available to you. Often, it may seem that the places and activities of interest to you and your friends are just not accessible any more. You and your friends should find new places to go that will meet your needs. In addition, it may be difficult to meet people because of feelings regarding your disability and the changes that you have experienced since your injury. How to overcome these feelings begins by developing interest and enthusiasm that can be shared and pursued in social situations. Make the best of your personal strengths in appearance, conversation, and social skills; set goals for your personal growth, and develop strategies to make yourself feel as good as you can about yourself.

12 I am gay/lesbian. How do I meet potential partners?

Because of advocacy efforts by gay men and lesbians, there are now many alternatives to the bar scene. Social groups, political action groups, and a variety of support groups are available in many cities. Support groups for gays or lesbians who have disabilities may be available at your local independent living center. In addition, resource guides are available in local bookstores. They list meetings, places, businesses, resorts, and host of other gay- and lesbian-oriented services and social affiliations. (See Appendix B for other information.)

13 How concerned should I be about accessibility to social meeting places?

Look for the options that work best for you. For example, if your favorite spot is inaccessible, is there another store or nightclub that you like that is more accessible? Are you willing to contact the management or a city agency and work toward improving the accessibility of this particular place? What will attitudes be like in a place that is not wheelchair accessible? Are you willing to work toward changing them? In the past, accessibility and accommodation for people who use wheelchairs was very poor. Now, however, with the passage of the Americans with Disabilities Act, public facilities must be accessible, and attitudes have begun to change.

It is more important than ever to think ahead and plan your activities before you find yourself in places and situations that may feel uncomfortable. You may want to call ahead and check out the accessibility and then make your decision. Your independent living center may also have directories of accessible locations and restaurants. You can talk to other people who have visited a place, or you may want to work with the center in performing accessibility surveys and developing a local directory if there is not one. Again, think ahead and ask yourself some important questions. How do I feel about being carried into a place? What is it like to accept assistance? Can I talk about my needs and work together with my partner if I find myself in a dicey situation?

14 How do I tell someone that I am interested in him/her?

Communication can be made less mysterious and assertiveness less daunting if we simplify it. Try to avoid playing games by remaining open, honest, and direct. It's not necessary to think of clever lines or more ways of attracting another person's attention.

Good relationships, dating, and eventually marriage often develop out of positive friendships. If you approach a potential relationship as you would a friendship, it can be less threatening and frightening. Seeing the person as a potential friend may help put you at ease and feel more relaxed. Let the person know that you are interested in spending time together, and invite the person to do something with you. This sounds simple, but in reality it may be difficult because of how vulnerable you feel when your emotions are on the line.

Try to be direct. In general, good assertive communication begins with the word "I." Try practicing with friends, and get as much support as possible from people who are close to you. Remember, this is something everyone has problems with. Expressing feelings that you have for another person is difficult for most people, but it can be very fulfilling and rewarding once you've been able to do it.

15 Should I date another person with a disability?

That depends on whom you feel attracted to and comfortable with. There is nothing wrong with dating another person with a disability, or in never doing this. If you do, you may require the services of a personal care attendant or someone else to assist you in activities such as undressing or getting into bed for sex. Dating another person with a disability can be very positive and may allow you to share personal feelings about yourself. Let your feelings lead you to trust your instincts. Choosing partners simply because they have a disability or don't may be the result of unresolved feelings about your own disability.

16 Are there special things to think about before getting involved in a relationship?

Getting into a relationship is often something that just happens and can't be planned. Nevertheless, it might be helpful to think about what is important to you in a relationship and to look for a partner who shares similar values and beliefs. For many people, open expressions of love, affection, trust, respect, and sensitivity are important. For others, it is important to find a partner who shares your feelings regarding sex, money, power, children, religion, and communication. Although some of these issues may not be important as you begin to date someone, they may become increasingly important as the relationship matures and becomes more serious. If the two of you share the same feelings and values from the beginning, there is certainly a better chance that you will grow close and that the relationship will last longer.

17 When should I tell a new partner about my injury?

Because spinal cord injury is highly visible, it is likely that you started talking about it from the beginning. It is always your decision as to how much you wish to reveal about yourself and the details of your injury and your feelings. You have a right to privacy, and you may feel that the issues around your injury are personal. If you decide to talk openly, it's wise not to overwhelm a partner with too many details at once. Take your clues from your partner. See how much information he or she would like about you. Answer questions as they arise, and keep lines of communication open.

If you and your partner are sexually attracted to each other, you might want to consider talking about your feelings and the practical aspects of sex. The more you share about your sexuality, the less you will feel anxious and tense during intimate times. Start slowly, communicate on an ongoing basis, and support your partner. This may be a new experience for the both of you, and supporting each other will be critical as you get closer.

18 Will someone want to stay with me in a long-term relationship?

There is no guarantee that any relationship has what it takes to survive over a long period of time. Even without disabilities, about 55% of all marriages in the United States end in divorce. Research, however, has demonstrated that relationships that begin after the onset of disability may be more stable than those begun before the disability occurred. If the relationship was faltering before the injury, chances are that the disability will not be the deciding factor in its survival. Your disability may require a period of adjustment for both of you. Keep the lines of communication open, and talk about all the adjustments that you have to make to allow the relationship to survive and to thrive.

19 How do I know if I am in love?

There is no simple answer to a question as complex as this one. There is no magic way to know that you are in love or that this is a good relationship for you. Love can creep up on you, or you may know it from the beginning. Love often involves taking a risk and putting yourself in a vulnerable situation with your feelings toward another person. If the relationship helps you to feel better about yourself and gives you positive feelings, it may be love. Give the relationship time, and let the two of you get close. Many people require feelings of safety and trust to get the most from sex, but sex and love are not the same thing. For some people, each can exist without the other. Trust your instincts and the voice inside you. They will tell you when to become intimate with your partner.

20 Can I still have a sex life?

A spinal cord injury changes your sexual options, but it does not prevent you from having a fulfilling sex life. You can still be a desirable and exciting sexual person. The necessary components of having a sex life include feeling good about yourself, knowing what you want sexually, and understanding how your body responds since your injury. Only you can decide how to express your sexuality and how to feel as good as possible about your looks and your body. Your partner may help improve your feelings of self-esteem, but these feelings come from inside and are your responsibility.

Everyone is capable of responding in a sexual manner. Explore your body to learn what works for you now. Ask yourself what you want to give and receive in a sexual relationship. When you have thought about all this, select a partner who has similar values and can give and receive in a compatible fashion. For now, you may choose to express your sexuality with yourself. There is nothing wrong with not being in a relationship. You can have a fulfilling and rich life as a single person with a support system of friends and relatives.

21 How often should I want to have sex?

There is no rule on how often people should want to have sex or how sexy people should feel. After a spinal cord injury, many people find that they have little interest in sex for many months. Often, if they don't have a partner, it may be very difficult to begin dating and to meet somebody with whom they feel comfortable. The important thing is to not become isolated and to face your fear as soon as possible, before it becomes overwhelming. Other people find that they want to be intimate with a partner or to masturbate as soon as possible after injury. Chances are that if sex was important to you before your injury, it will continue to be important to you after injury. If it was not important then, you probably won't feel like having sex very often now. Again, there is no right or wrong answer to questions like this.

22 I've never had sex. What will it be like?

There is no formula for sex. Everyone has different fantasies about what sex may be like. To a large extent, these fantasies are based on our history and our needs at a particular time. Most people need to feel a degree of physical attraction to another individual. Many need to feel emotionally connected and to trust the other person. Most people prefer a quiet, comfortable setting where there is little chance of interruption as they become physically familiar with one another.

People vary tremendously as to how they give and receive pleasure and arousal. While many people equate sex with intercourse, real sexual contact is any exchange of intimacies, whether physical or emotional. Foreplay implies kissing, caressing, stroking, or licking. But that choice is better left to the couple themselves.

Orgasm is not a requirement of lovemaking or sexual stimulation. Having an orgasm during lovemaking depends on the preference, mood, physical capacity, and values of each partner. Some people expect orgasm, even simultaneous orgasms, for themselves and their partner. Others do not. It is best to learn what works best for you and what makes you and your partner feel the most comfortable.

Sex can be exciting, regardless of whether you had sexual experiences before your injury. If you had no experiences before your injury, this may be a time of anxiety, excitement, unexpected pleasures, and discovery, just as it is for people without injuries. Try to discuss your feelings with your partner and begin slowly. Use the first time to explore your body and your partner's. Try not to focus on intercourse or orgasm. Instead, try to enjoy the sensations of being touched and giving pleasure to your partner.

23 Why am I not interested in sex anymore?

The level of interest in sexuality is different for each person, and it may change from time to time throughout life. If your injury is recent, it may take some time before you are ready to start dating and become intimate with another person. There is nothing wrong with this. Feelings of sadness, anxiety, and discomfort about your body may all contribute to an overall decrease in your sex drive.

Sometimes negative experiences or even physical factors may be responsible for your lack of interest. Do you fantasize? Do you enjoy it, or does it upset you? Have you ever been hurt or abused in a sexual way? Have you received negative messages about your sexuality? Depending on how disturbing and long-lasting your lack of sexual interest is, you might want to pursue evaluation (gynecological, endocrine, or psychological) to identify the cause and to undertake possible treatment.

Some people may choose not to be sexual. If you choose not to be sexual, try to understand the reasons behind your decision. Is it a decision of strength or a decision based on fear, poor self-esteem, feelings of shame, or intimidation? Sometimes, people can believe that they are not interested in sex when they are really afraid of the intimacy and vulnerability that often go along with it. Being sexually active can be difficult for anyone because of vulnerability, fears of rejection, and concerns about showing our naked bodies to another person. If you share some of these feelings, go slowly but try to take steps toward feeling positive about yourself. The rewards will be well worth it.

Remember, though, that there is nothing wrong with you if you decide not to be sexually active or if you find that you have little interest in sex. This may change over time as your emotional situation changes. Or you may find that you have other interests instead of sex. Actually, there can be many reasons why a person is not interested in sex, and you don't owe an explanation to anyone. You have a right to your own feelings. Even if you decide not to be sexually active, however, you can still experience intimacy through kissing, touching, and hugging. Masturbation is also an option.

24 Is it normal to worry about sex so much?

In general, most people think a lot about sex, especially if there have been changes that may affect their sex life. Some experts believe that at least 50% of the population have diffi-culties associated with sex and see themselves as having a sexual problem. Researchers have found that sex is one of the primary concerns of most people with a spinal cord in-jury. Worries about sex are more frequent than concerns about walking. There is no right or wrong. Each person wor-ries about different things. If you find that your worries about sex are making it difficult for you to think about other things or are interfering in your day-to-day life, you might want to think about talking with a peer counselor or some-one else you trust. For most of us, talking about our worries is a good way to solve problems or find answers.

25 I feel so passive now. How can I really be sexual?

Although you are probably reacting to changes in your mo-bility, these feelings of being passive are psychological in na-ture. You may feel disconnected from your experience be-cause it's so different from it was before your injury. You may also be experiencing feelings of embarrassment and having difficulty depending on another person. In any case, these feelings are probably temporary and can be changed with a lot of hard work on your part. It will be important in your general adjustment to feel in control and to be active rather than passive with your sexuality.

Surveys of women with spinal cord injuries who have adjusted well sexually have found that they have become more independent, assertive, and active as sexual partners. These women have acknowledged that the first few years after injury were difficult and extremely stressful. As they became more secure in their identity, they were better able to adjust sexually as well. A good starting place is to take control whenever possible and to be active in as many deci-sions as possible. Start with the small things that feel more comfortable and safe. As you master the ability to make deci-sions and be assertive, you will find that your self-esteem

and feelings about yourself will also improve. Like everything, this takes some time and is a gradual process. Sometimes, it's hard to see the progress you may be making. Get
as much support as possible from friends, family, peer counselor, and health care providers you can trust.

26   How can I feel like a man again?

A spinal cord injury doesn't take away from your manhood.
Nevertheless, it is common for men to feel unsure about
themselves. Look inward and give some thought to what
makes you a man. Even though we often thing of our muscles, our bodies, physical activities, and our sex organs, they
are only the symbols of our manhood. Masculinity goes
much deeper and has been a part of us long before we ma-
tured and grew up. Our masculinity is expressed in everything we do and say. It's a part of our personality and how
we relate to other people. It doesn't have to change after a
spinal cord injury.

27   How can I feel more sexy?

People with and without disabilities may experience doubts
about their sexual self-concept and have periods of lack of
desire. Feeling better about yourself often entails changing
messages about your sexuality that you have taken in over
the years. Try to understand how the negative messages began. How did you develop feelings about yourself that were
unhealthy and undesirable? Often people are not even aware
of negative feelings—sadness, guilt, anger, and anxiety—

regarding sexuality that they have accumulated over the years. They may have come from the media, religion, parents, teachers, or any number of people. By identifying these messages, we are able to understand them and express them so that they don't interfere with our relationships and our sexual activity. By repressing these negative feelings, we often act as if they were true. We can easily sabotage a relationship and repeat cycles of self-doubt and self-blame. It is a liberating experience to realize that we have control over our relationship, how we are treated, and how we feel about ourselves.

Sensuality exercises are also useful in helping people feel more sexual and in touch with their senses. Begin by focusing on the positive aspects of yourself and the parts of you that you feel good about. Perhaps others can help point out some of the positive aspects of your personality and your appearance. Try to deepen these feelings and explore the positive aspects of you and your relationships. If you are not in a relationship, try not to let that affect how you feel about yourself. All too often people feel incomplete without a partner. People without partners are still sexual beings. They still have dreams and fantasies about sex. They still have feelings. They are still sexual regardless of whether they use their bodies in sexual activities.

28 Will I develop sexually like my friends?

Sexual development for boys and girls is a complex process that entails physical and psychological factors. On a physical basis, a spinal cord injury will not affect sexual maturation. The body will develop at the same time as young people who do not have spinal cord injury. Physically, however, your body may respond differently to sexual stimulation, and it can be confusing and frightening. Psychologically, sexual development requires access to sound information, opportunities for experimentation, social skills, self-awareness, and knowledge of sexual opportunities available to you.

Parental attitudes toward sexuality are important as young people develop a sexual identity and begin to explore their sexual behaviors. Typically, young people who have a disability are overprotected in these areas and are deprived of important social opportunities for interacting with the opposite sex. The teenage and young-adult years are a critical time for sexual development. If you have concerns in this area, consider talking with parents, peers, or professionals who provide information and education.

29 How do I tell my parents about my sexual activity?

The first decision is to determine whether it is necessary to tell your parents about your sexual activity. If you are an adult, you have the right to privacy regarding your sexuality. Adults generally don't share the details of their sexual activity with their parents, nor do parents tell their children about their sexual behavior. If you have a close and open relationship with your parents, chances are that they will respect your feelings and desires. If your relationship is not so close, you may want to tell them that you need more privacy and that you have a right to explore whatever sexual relationships that are available to you. You may also need to remind them that having a disability does not detract from your sexuality—that your sexual needs are as real now as they ever were. Parents often have difficulty recognizing the sexual needs of their children.

In you have recently moved home since your injury, good communication with your parents regarding sexuality and other issues may be critical. There is no easy way to speak with parents about such personal and sensitive issues. Tell them what you need; reassure them that you can make your own decisions and that you will take responsibility for your choices. If it appears that your presence in their home means feeling overly dependent on them and adjusting to rules that do not seem fair, you may want to contact your local independent living center for other options regarding housing and personal care services.

30 Can someone become a homosexual as a result of an injury?

No, people do not change their sexual orientation after a spinal cord injury. Little is actually known about what determines our sexual preferences, whether it is caused by genetic or environmental factors. But regardless of how sexual orientation develops, it does not change after a traumatic event such as an injury. If you were homosexual before the injury, you will continue to feel attracted to members of your own gender. If you were heterosexual before your injury, you will have the same feelings afterward.

31 How do I know if I am a homosexual?

Lesbians are women who love and are sexually attracted to other women. Gay men are men who love and are sexually attracted to other men. Coming out is a process of recognizing and affirming one's identity. Some people at first deny their attraction to individuals of the same sex because of their own, their family's, or society's negative stereotypes. We live in a homophobic culture—one that irrationally fears and hates homosexuality in ourselves or other people—and the process of coming out sometimes involves dealing with feelings of guilt, self-hatred, and fear. It may help you to know that being a homosexual is not a choice. It is a natural way of being for about 5% of the population. You can choose to express your sexuality or not. You may come out at any stage or age during your life. Frequently, the process of coming out involves getting to know other gay men or lesbians, deciding how to tell other people, and possibly becoming active in the gay rights movement.

32 What is it like to be gay or lesbian and have a spinal cord injury?

Spinal cord injures happen to all people regardless of sexual orientation. If you are gay or lesbian and have a spinal cord injury, you can expect the same ignorance and biases that you have always encountered. Rehabilitation centers and the medical profession in general are not equipped to handle people who fall outside the mainstream of society. People may be rude to you at times, ignore special requests that you may have, or find it difficult to relate to your partner. You may, for example, have to insist that your partner be trained in your self-care activities, transfers, and medical requirements. You may find yourself shunned by other rehabilitation patients in the hospital and have to demand that your rights be respected.

You and your partner, however, will have the same sexual options available to you as before. Gay men may need to consider erection aids or other devices in order to maintain erections. Like all men with a spinal cord injury, there may be difficulties with ejaculation and orgasm, but this will depend on the nature of your spinal cord injury. Some individuals have reported that the gay and lesbian communities can be very supportive and helpful, while others have said the opposite. To some extent, it will depend on how you present yourself to others and how you feel about yourself.

33 How does a person communicate about sex?

Talking about sex is often difficult since it is such a private matter. It is easy to become embarrassed or feel very sensitive about your feelings. Yet it is one of the most important aspects of any relationship and necessary for your own emotional well-being. Time your discussion carefully; try to find times that you will not be disturbed or when you are not upset about other issues. Keep your conversation to the topic and don't bring other issues into the discussions. Talk about yourself rather than trying to tell the other person how he or she feels. This will help reduce defensiveness and allow your partners the freedom to talk about themselves. Never assume anything in a discussion of this nature. No one is a mind reader. Each point should be clearly stated until the other person is sure that he or she understands. Make sure that what you have heard is actually what your partner has said. Check it out by repeating it and asking, "Is this what you mean?"

34 How important is sex in a relationship?

That depends. For most people, sexual expression is a critical component of a relationship. This is true not only for the obvious physical pleasure associated with sex, but also because of the emotional intimacy. The importance of sexual expression may change in your mind during your life, and its importance may change in your relationship as well. Chances are, though, that some form of intimacy will always be an important part of your significant relationships.

35 Will my partner still be turned on?

Whether a partner finds it enjoyable to have sex with you depends on you and your partner. Your attitudes and your partner's attitudes about your disability play an important role in the quality of your sexual relationship. Sex is not about performance or the best techniques. It is about pleasure, sharing, and communicating feelings.

There are many ways the two of you can find to give and receive pleasure, regardless of physical limitations. You can stimulate each other with words and looks, touching and rubbing various parts of your bodies irrespective of the amount of movement or sensation that you happen to have in any given area. For women, even if vaginal stimulation causes you problems, his penis can still be rubbed between your legs or breasts or in your mouth. If your finger movements do not allow you to stroke his penis, you can deliver intense stimulation with a vibrator. For men, regardless of whether you have an erection, your partner may find pleasure in rubbing his or her genitals on various parts of your body. Use words, your mouth, or your hands to give pleasure. Find out what each of you prefers and is willing to provide. Are there sexual games that the two of you could enjoy? Learn to be effective sexual partners with one another and worry less about being an ideal partner.

36 I want to have sex, but my partner has lost interest. What should I do?

It is not unusual for a couple to experience times of stress and tension when a trauma such as a spinal cord injury takes place. This is a difficult event for both of you. As always, the most important step is to begin talking about the distance that you are feeling in the relationship. Make sure that your lover is not providing your medical care and that he or she still feels special and important to you. The adjustment to injury is a slow process that, in many ways, can't be hurried. Give the relationship time and get to know one another again. Be as sociable with each other as you were when you first met. Go out to dinner and give each other a chance to get used to the changes that have occurred. Get to know each other again instead of pretending that neither of you has changed and that life has continued on as normal. Be sincere, open, and nondefensive.

Try to be honest and look inside yourself as well. Have you been attentive to your partner? Have you been so self-absorbed that his or her needs and wants have gone unnoticed? Have you been romantic and expressed your intimate feelings to your partner? Have you made the other person feel special, or have you been demanding and irritable? Have you been depressed and feeling sorry for yourself? Yes, you have the right to these feelings, but your partner may be reacting to the messages that you are conveying. No one is 100% to blame for all the difficulties in a relationship. Correcting your share may be a critical step in addressing some of the problems.

Sometimes a lack of interest in sex may indicate a serious problem in your relationship. If communication has broken down, it may be time to think about seeing a professional for some relationship counseling. Remember, though, that the problems may be simple and transient—a period of stress at work, say, that has your partner temporarily preoccupied. Don't jump to conclusions that the problems have to do with your partner's feelings toward you or that you are no longer attractive to your partner. Support each other as much as possible during this time, and keep the lines of communication open.

37   How do I say no to my partner?

Some of the most difficult times regarding sex are when one person wants more than the other. But let's get real. There are times when you are not going to feel like having sex and doing so will only make you feel resentful. At these times, try to be as honest as possible, saying something like, "I am sorry if this disappoints you, but I'm not in the mood."

Sometimes people, with or without a spinal cord injury, feel that they must have sex to keep their partner happy or to keep the relationship going. As a result, it may be difficult to express your true feelings. Saying "no" may hurt your lover, but it may also strengthen your relationship in the long run.

38   Is there anything I can do to make sex better?

The exciting parts of sex are different for each of us, but there may be some things that will add to the pleasure. First, try having sex during the day or when the lights are on. This will add to the sensual experience of sex and will help to compensate for decreases in feeling that you may have in your body. Try to talk about your feelings and what feels good or bad during sex. Again, doing this over time can really help to enhance your pleasure and can be a real turn-on. Describe what you would like your partners to do and tell them how it feels. Share your fantasies and take your time. Enjoy touching and being touched. Get into kissing, touching, intimate talk, and experimentation. Find out how your body works now and discover how your sexual pleasure can be intensified. Finally, use different parts of your body for sensuous and sexual pleasure. Where is the sensation the greatest? Where does it feel the best? Try having your nipples touched and kissed. Your neck, hair, ears, nose, and finger tips may all be sources of pleasure. Try to let your inhibitions down and enjoy the emotional and physical aspects of being close. The only rules for sex are that you both agree on what you are doing and that no one is being hurt.

39 Will his penis fall out of my vagina during intercourse?

If your injury results in lack of muscle control around the vagina, it could be somewhat loose for your partner's penis. Kegel exercises can tighten the muscles if you can voluntarily contract and release the muscles. Simply squeeze the same muscles that you use to control the flow of urine when you urinate. Some experimental medicines have also helped in cases where there is loose vaginal entry without muscle control. In general, however, a firm penis is not going to fall out. The skill of your partner in moving against you and changes in position are all that is needed. If you can form a circle with your fingers, you can increase the stimulation he receives by sliding the penis through the "finger ring" as it enters the vagina. He could also add extra stimulation himself by using his fingers around the penis while having intercourse. Again, creating options for both of you is the best way to resolve potential problems. The fear of his penis falling out is more of a psychological issue that should be discussed before beginning sexual activity.

40 Will my vagina be tight enough for my partner to enjoy intercourse?

This is a common worry for women after a spinal cord injury, after childbirth, or both. Sometimes, an area is affected by an injury, and the muscles are not as tight as before. The vagina, however, expands to fit the size of the penis inserted into it. Therefore, even though the sensation may be different for your partner, there will be friction between the walls of the vagina and the penis. If you have control of the pubococcygeus muscle (which controls the flow of urine), you can achieve much better tone by regular exercise of the muscle. If you do not have control of this muscle, check with your doctor. This area is constantly being researched, and new developments are currently being studied.

41 I have not engaged in sex for years. Can I be sexually active now?

There is absolutely no reason why a period of abstinence should prevent you from functioning sexually. When you resume sexual activity, though, take it slow and get comfortable with yourself and with your partner. There may be some anxiety after a long abstinence. If this happens, try talking with your partner and sharing some of your feelings. It may help reduce the tension and encourage your partner to give you support as you proceed.

42 What should I do if my partner becomes abusive?

The physical abuse of women has reached epidemic proportions in the United States. The only way to stop the violence is to leave the situation immediately. It is important to remember that you are not to blame for the violence and battering. No matter how much neater, sexier, better, or quieter you are, you cannot change an abusive mate. An abusive relationship does severe damage to your self-esteem, making it very difficult to leave the relationship. People who are abused can easily begin to feel that they deserve the abuse. They often fear that they will not be able to find another partner and that this abusive relationship is better than none at all.

Women with spinal cord injury, who may be more dependent on their mates and who may have lower self-esteem, can have greater difficulty in leaving abusive relationships. Most communities have shelters where counseling and safety are provided to battered women. In addition, independent living programs can be helpful in finding alternative housing or personal care services. If there is ever danger of being hurt in an abusive relationship, the woman always has the option of calling the police to ensure her safety. A restraining order may be necessary to keep your abuser a safe distance from you. Even with a restraining order, however, the woman needs to be cautious and aware of her safety.

43 Can a man be sexually abused?

Yes, both men and women can be victims of sexual abuse. As a person with a disability, in fact, you may be vulnerable to such an attack. Generally, people with disabilities have a higher incidence of abuse than people without disabilities. No one deserves to be the victim of abuse, and it is important to end an abusive relationship no matter how important the person is to you. Sometimes, care providers or other people that you trust may take advantage of you or cause you emotional or physical harm. Should this happen, remove yourself from danger as soon as possible, and report them to the authorities immediately.

44 Should I go to a prostitute?

Hiring a prostitute after your injury is a personal decision that only you can make. It often seems like an easy solution to a difficult problem. Many who have tried it, however, have found the experience disappointing and unrewarding. The lack of emotional bonding can make the entire encounter cold and painful.

Although it may take more time to develop real relationships, it is an important step in rebuilding self-esteem after an injury. Start slowly and let the sexual relationship unfold gradually. Don't expect to be a great lover immediately.

If you do decide to see a prostitute, be very careful about sexually transmitted diseases and use every precaution possible. Realize also that prostitution is illegal and you run the risk of arrest.

45 Can I ever get married?

Having a spinal cord injury is no reason not to get married. The rate of marriage for people with spinal cord injury is about the same as it is for the general population, although it tends to occur later in life. Generally, these marriages are more stable too; spouses report that they are pleased with their relationships and enjoy positive sexual relations. Divorce rates tend to be lower for people who marry after their injury, and these relationships seem to be mature and healthy.

How soon should you get married after a spinal cord injury?

Many people make the mistake of rushing into marriage right after their spinal cord injury. Some marriages have been performed in the rehabilitation centers shortly after the injury. These "rushed" marriages generally have a poor chance for success and tend to happen because of fears and rejections. If you were planning to be married before your injury, try to give both of you as much time as possible to absorb the consequences of your injury and the changes that have occurred in your relationship. This may mean waiting a year or two. If you can wait that long, your marriage will be stronger and many of the necessary adjustments will have already occurred. Getting married soon after injury is often very stressful because the two of you will be dealing with the adjustments of the injury while you are also dealing with the changes of married life. Studies have shown that these marriages tend not to last.

Do marriages last after a spinal cord injury? My spouse feels like my nurse. Is that normal?

A spinal cord injury will create a great deal of stress for you and your spouse. Many marriages do last after an injury, but some cannot adapt. If you are able to discuss your feelings, remain sensitive to the feelings of your partner, and develop a positive attitude toward the future, your marriage will have a much greater likelihood of lasting. Feeling sorry for yourself and taking anger out on your partner, unfortunately, are common reactions after an injury and can inspire resentment and a sense of helplessness. More than ever, your relationship will require teamwork and mutual support. This can be a time to get closer to each other rather than further apart.

48 When should people see a marriage counselor?

Unfortunately, most couples tend to wait until there is a crisis in their relationship before deciding to see a marriage counselor. Often, this may be too late, and the couple may have drifted apart. A marriage counselor can be helpful at any time in a relationship. Also, you don't need to be married to see a counselor. Many people seek a counselor to discuss changes in a relationship or to find solutions to difficult problems that the couple may be facing. If the two of you are having a stressful time, you may want to talk things over with a third person. A counselor may be a psychologist or social worker at the rehabilitation center, but you can also find helpful professionals at many community agencies. If possible, find someone who has experience working with a person who has a physical disability. It makes the whole process much smoother.

49 How will my sex life change as I get older?

Your sexuality is an important part of life from birth to death. As a person gets older, the quality of sexual expressions may become better than ever. In the last decades of life, many people remain sexually active and enjoy sexual pleasures as often as they did earlier in life. Others may tend to decrease their activity because of diseases, disabilities, the lack of a partner, or because they have lost some interest in sex.

Regardless of the level of your activity, there may be some physical changes that will affect your functioning. If you are a man, your erections may be less firm, and if you were able to ejaculate and reach orgasms these may be less powerful than they were. Also, you may need to wait longer periods of time between sexual activities in order to become aroused.

Physically, the major change that many women report as they get older is decreased lubrication after menopause. Regular sexual activity may compensate for this and keep tissues of the vagina healthy. Because of your injury, you may have already noticed a decrease in lubrication. This does not mean that your body is aging more rapidly. Rather it is a function of the nerve blockage in the spinal cord. You may also note reduced strength and stamina as you get older. As a result, positions and scheduling of sexual activity may need to be adjusted to take advantage of times when you feel the best. Some women, as they get older, also report a slow-down in their sexual drive. This may be the result of a hormone change or harmful stereotypes about the sexuality of older women in our culture.

Today, there is much research on the effects of aging and of spinal cord injury. Little is actually known, however, about the sexual aspects of aging for a person with spinal cord injury. If your sexual abilities have changed since you became older, this may be the time to consider medical intervention. If you are interested in staying active, there are many options that medical professionals can provide that may assist your lovemaking.

The most important aspect of sexuality that changes with aging is often your attitude. Sex in the context of a long-term relationship can still be vital and fulfilling despite the fact that it isn't new and surprising. Couples who explore the depth and richness of their emotional and spiritual connection find that sex actually may get better with age.

50 Is there such a thing as male menopause?

Many people feel that male menopause causes physical or emotional changes to occur. Male menopause is usually marked by the transition from one development stage to another, such as from early adulthood to middle age. It can happen for men as well as women. Sex drive varies from one man to another, and many men remain sexually active until they reach their seventies or eighties. Other men find a gradual decrease in their sex drive as they become older. Emotional changes are also common during menopause. There may be mood swings or periods of depression and feelings of loss. They usually will pass as you adapt to the changes in your life. If they persist or if they seem severe, a professional counselor can often help you understand the basis for your sadness and depression.

51 Is it true that women stop having sex after menopause?

No. Women, like men, are never too old to enjoy sex. Women stop having periods after menopause, but they do not stop engaging in sexual activities. As a result of menopause, the walls of the vagina tend to dry out, causing an irritation during intercourse. Unless this is treated with artificial lubricants or hormone creams, sexual intercourse can be painful. Some women report that their sex drive decreases at menopause, while others say that their drive increases with age. It is not clear whether this is caused by physical or psychological factors. Often older women stop having sex because of health-related problems or because of the lack of available partners. In general, it is believed that regular sexual activity for women is healthy and beneficial to the genitals. Regular sex tends to keep the vagina moist and pelvic muscles in shape.

52

Will I need hormone replacement therapy when I go through menopause?

Menopause or "change of life" is a process that symbolizes the ending of a woman's ability to become pregnant. Starting around 40 years old, the amount of female hormone, estrogen, begins to decrease in the body. Your periods may become irregular and over a period of years will stop altogether. This is a result of very low estrogen levels that are no longer capable of triggering your periods. The point between when your periods stop and the year after is called menopause. The average age for this is about 52, but it's different for each woman. To some extent, the age at which menopause begins is hereditary, so that you may be able to determine roughly when to expect this change from speaking with your mother and grandmother. Although menopause will signify the end of your reproductive years, it isn't the end of your life. The average life expectancy for women today is approximately 78 years, so that about one third of a woman's life occurs after menopause.

Some women have very few symptoms before, during, and after menopause. Other women suffer severe difficulties, including irritability, insomnia, hot flashes, vaginal dryness, mood swings, and heart palpitations. If these symptoms are severe enough, hormone replacement therapy may be suggested. Not only does it minimize the symptoms, it also produces positive effects on bone density and cholesterol levels. It also reduces the risk of stroke and heart disease. Some women are afraid of trying hormone replacement therapy because there was some evidence that it increased the risk of breast cancer. Newer research, however, has proven this connection to be false, and now estrogen is being given in combination with another hormone, progestin (synthetic progesterone). For women who have a history of heart disease, stroke, smoking, breast cancer, fibroids, and other medical conditions, doctors tend not to recommend hormone replacement therapy. Instead, menopause symptoms are handled through an exercise program, diet, and herbal medicines.

The entire issue of menopause in women who have spinal cord injury is not well understood. Little research has been done, and scientists are just not aware of how the injury affects this normal process of life. Federal health agencies have identified this as an area that must be addressed and have made it a research priority.

3 Physical Aspects

1. Does cigarette smoking affect erections?

2. Will smoking marijuana or drinking alcohol affect my sex life?

3. What drugs interfere with sex?

4. Are there drugs to make me feel sexually aroused?

5. Are there medications or hormones that will improve my erections?

6. Will a head injury affect my sex life too?

7. Is my erection problem caused by depression or poor self-esteem?

8. How will I know if I am turned on if I don't have an erection?

9. How come I get hard when I wash my penis or get catheterized but I can't keep the erection?

10. What is a reflex erection?

11. What is stuffing?

12. Why does my penis curve or have a bend in it?

13. If I put a rubber band on the base of my penis, will it stay hard? Is it safe to do this?

14. Where can I get a penis ring?

15. How do vacuum devices work to give an erection?

16. How do I use a vacuum device when I have limited use of my hands?

17. Are most men satisfied using a vacuum device?

18. Can there be complications from using a vacuum device?

19. Can I still use a vacuum device if I have had an implant in the past or if I use an injection program?

20. What types of penile implants are available?

21. Should I get a penile implant?

22. Are implants permanent?

23. What kind of side effects can develop from an implant?

24. What is papaverine?

25. Will a penile injection program allow me to have a climax and ejaculation?

26. Are there side effects from using a penile injection program?

27. Is there surgery that can improve my erections?

28. Is it normal to have erection problems as you get older?

29. How important is penis size?

30. Is masturbation normal?

31. Can I masturbate after injury?

32. Can I hurt myself if I masturbate too much?

33. Is there anything wrong with using a vibrator?

34. Do men ever use vibrators?

35. Is it dangerous to use a vibrator?

36. Do women have fantasies? About what? What about wet dreams?

37. How can a woman masturbate?

38. Do I still become lubricated after a spinal cord injury?

39. Where is my clitoris?

40. What is my G spot?

41. Will I ever have an orgasm again?

42. What is an emotional orgasm?

43. Can I come more than once?

44. Why do I have an erection but don't ejaculate?

45. How do I explain my bladder and bowel to a new partner?

46. Should I have sex when I have a bladder infection?

47. What do I do with my leg bag?

48. What if I urinate during sex?

49. Can I have sex with a catheter in place?

50. Can I have sex with a suprapubic tube in place?

51. Can I minimize the chance of bowel accident?

52. What if I have a bowel movement during sex?

53. Is there any way that I can increase the pleasure of being touched if I don't have sensation in my body?

54. How can I get pleasure when I can't feel in my vagina?

55. My skin feels hypersensitive sometimes. What should I do?

56. Pain interferes with my sexual desire. What can I do?

57. How can I be sexually active if I am in pain?

58. Since I can't feel anything, will my partner hurt me during sex?

59. Will intercourse hurt?

60. What if I have spasms during sex?

61. How do I get ready for sex?

62. How can I reduce the anxiety before sex?

63. Where can I have sex now?

64. Can I have sex in my wheelchair?

65. How will my partner transfer me into bed?

66. I can't use the same sexual positions as before my accident. What positions will work for a woman?

67. What positions work best for a man?

68. Can I still be on top during sex?

69. Is there a right way to have intercourse?

1 Does cigarette smoking affect erections?

After a spinal cord injury, the primary cause of erection problems is damage to the nerve pathways in the spinal cord. But cigarette smoking can cause additional problems because of its effect on blood flow. Nicotine in the body tends to restrict blood flow by constricting small blood vessels in the penis, making erections less rigid. Also, cigarette smoking has many adverse effects on other systems of the body that are essential for good health, especially after an injury.

2 Will smoking marijuana or drinking alcohol affect my sex life?

Alcohol is a depressant and will make sexual functioning even more difficult. Smoking marijuana may improve your fantasy life, but it can have negative effects as well. It can raise your anxiety level and make communication more difficult. Both can make you less attractive to your partner. Nevertheless, drinking in a responsible manner is socially acceptable and can be a part of your social life as long as it is safe, given the medications you are taking. It is best, however, to be yourself and discuss any feelings that you may have with your partner.

3 What drugs interfere with sex?

Many drugs prescribed for people with spinal cord injury can interfere with sexual functioning. These include anticholinergics, antidepressants, antispasmodics, antihypertensives, and anticonvulsants. In many men, these drugs reduce the ability to achieve erection or ejaculation. They can also reduce sexual desire and cause depression and fatigue. When starting new medication, it is always a good idea to talk with your doctor regarding the possible side effects of the medication and see if your medication will affect your sexual expression. At times, medicine can be changed to alternatives that will have little or no effect on your sex life. At other times, changes in the dosage may decrease the impact of the medication on your ability to function sexually.

Research on drug effects and women with spinal cord injury is woefully incomplete. Not many studies have been conducted, and few researchers are aware of the special problems shared by women with disabilities. There is some evidence, however, that alpha and beta blockers, antipsychotic medications, and antidepressants may delay or prevent women from experiencing orgasm. Sexual drive also may be reduced by medications that are often used by women who have spinal cord injury. However, Dantrium (dantrolene sodium), Lioresal (baclofen USP), and Valium (diazepam) do not interfere with lubrication or muscle contraction in the vaginal area. Specific questions regarding medications you are currently taking should be directed toward your doctors and pharmacist.

If you are taking birth control pills, you should know that a variety of prescription medications can reduce the effectiveness of these pills. PCP and marijuana can cause hormonal and menstrual changes. Cocaine, heroin, and methadone can also affect the central nervous system and interfere with sexual response in both sexes. Finally, alcohol will interfere with sexual drive and reduce the experience of orgasm. Street drugs and alcohol can cause sexual dysfunction in all women.

4 Are there drugs to make me feel sexually aroused?

In both males and females, the male hormone, testosterone, is responsible for desire. Physicians do not prescribe testosterone to women to stimulate desire, because of the masculine side effects it could create. There are no true aphrodisiacs for women. If you are generally healthy, there is probably no hormonal reason for lack of desire.

5 Are there medications or hormones that will improve my erections?

Prescribed medications, such as yohimbine, as well as injections of the hormone testosterone can increase the desire for sex and the quality of erections if testosterone levels are low. These generally are not effective after a spinal cord injury. Your erection problem is most likely the result of an interruption of nerve impulses to the penis, not hormone deficiencies. Even though this may not be an effective treatment for your particular problem, you may want to speak with a urologist or endocrinologist if you have any questions.

6 Will a head injury affect my sex life too?

It is not uncommon for people with spinal cord injuries also to have a head injury as a result of their accidents. Head injuries also affect sexual functioning, but in a different way than a spinal cord injury. Most often a head injury will affect your ability to communicate, your memory, your thinking, or your ability to express feelings. People with head injuries may also find that they have little interest in sex or that they act too quickly before they have a chance to think about the consequences. At other times, it may be difficult to control your temper, or you may cry easily. Partners also may find it difficult to know what to expect since behavior can be unpredictable after head injury. If you or your partner has a head injury in addition to a spinal cord injury, it may be a good idea to talk with a neurologist about the sexual implications of your injury. Remember that not all neurologists may feel comfortable discussing sexuality, and it may take time to find a person who can provide accurate answers to your questions.

7 Is my erection problem caused by depression or poor self-esteem?

If you are having a difficult time emotionally, it may affect your desire for sex or ability to be with other people. When we are depressed, we tend to want to be alone and often withdraw from others. We have little interest in doing things and don't have the energy to interact with friends or family. All of these factors affect who we are as sexual entities.

Chances are that your erection problem is a result of a neurological or physical cause, not depression and your emotional situation. Although these emotional reactions can affect erection quality, you have a medical condition that is causing the erection problem. There has been a disruption in the nerve pathways between your brain and your penis. Even though you feel turned on, the message is unable to reach your penis, so you don't get the response you once did.

8 How will I know if I am turned on if I don't have an erection?

Seeing and experiencing an erection is one of the ways that many men know that they are sexually aroused. However, arousal begins in the brain, not in the penis. Before your injury, this feeling was transmitted to your penis through your spinal cord and you got an erection. Now that there has been an injury, the message becomes blocked before it reaches the genitals. But other signs in your body may indicate that you are feeling aroused. These happened before your injury as well, but you tended not to notice them because you were more focused on your penis. Other physical signs that you are turned on may include an increased heart rate, tenderness in your nipples, changes in your breathing, and a general feeling of flushness. All of these are important signals that hormonal changes are occurring in our bodies and that we are becoming aroused.

One mistake to avoid is assuming that you are not aroused because you do not have an erection. People that fall into this trap report that they have little interest in sex and have lost their desire. Recognizing new feelings related to sexual excitement, however, takes time and relearning. Be patient with yourself.

9 How come I get hard when I wash my penis or get catheterized but I can't keep the erection?

There are different kinds of erections. After a spinal cord injury, you may be experiencing what is called a reflex erection. This type of erection may occur when your penis is being touched, even in a nonsexual way. But the erection usually lasts only as long as you continue to be touched or stimulated. This kind of erection has nothing to do with how aroused you may feel, and you generally have little control over how long it will last. This erection is not very reliable for sex, although with time and practice you and your partner may learn where to touch in order to sustain the erection. This type of erection is more common for men with quadriplegia, and the quality of the erection may vary from one person to another.

10   What is a reflex erection?

Some men with spinal cord injuries are capable of achieving a reflex-stimulated erection. These men tend to be those with higher level injuries, such as quadriplegia rather than paraplegia. A reflex erection is caused by either nonsexual or sexual stimulation of the penis or genital area. The stimulation may be from bed sheets, touch, a full bladder, or rubbing of the penis on clothing. Unlike regular erections, there is no relationship between a reflex erection and the level of sexual excitement. When the stimulation is removed, the erection will disappear. Therefore, reflex erections are often not satisfying for intercourse. They can even be a source of frustration and confusion. With practice, however, the couple can develop techniques to make these erections last for prolonged periods of time.

11   What is stuffing?

This is a technique in which the man stuffs his flaccid penis into a woman's vagina. Sometimes it is done to increase the physical stimulation on the penis and perhaps cause an erection. Most times, however, it is done to provide pleasure to a woman by giving her the sensation of having a penis in her vagina. It is often pleasurable for both partners.

12 Why does my penis curve or have a bend in it?

Peyronie disease is a medical condition that can often result in a curvature or bending of the penis. Often it can be so severe and painful that it is impossible to have intercourse even with a full erection. Peyronie disease is often caused by damage within the penis brought on by an injury to this area of the body. If you sustained trauma to your genital area when you got hurt, you may notice a change in the shape of your penis. There are treatments ranging from prescription creams to surgery that can sometimes be helpful.

13 If I put a rubber band on the base of my penis, will it stay hard? Is it safe to do this?

A penis ring traps the blood inside the penis and maintains the erection for as long as the ring is in place. Often, men have intercourse with the ring in place. You may, however, notice that the penis begins to turn blue or purple and feels cold to the touch. If you can ejaculate, you may not be able to with the ring in place. You will now notice that the sperm drips out of the penis when the ring is removed. These reactions are normal. The ring should not do any damage to the penis unless it is left on for too long. Doctors suggest that a penis ring not be left in place for more than 30 minutes. It is best to check with your urologist before using a device such as a ring.

14 Where can I get a penis ring?

Rings are usually in porno/sex shops in most large cities. In addition, you may be able to get them from advertisements in the back of some of the more popular men's magazines, such as *Penthouse, Hustler,* and *Playboy.* The safest way, however, is to see your urologist and have a ring prescribed as part of a vacuum erection device. The ring may be more effective in holding your erection if you use it in conjunction with a vacuum device. Your doctor can also tell you how to use it safely without worry of complications or damage to your penis.

15 How do vacuum devices work to give an erection?

The vacuum constriction device is the safest, least expensive, and probably the most widely used technique to improve erections. A vacuum tube is placed over the penis, and an erection is created by pumping air out and thus drawing blood into the penis. A ring is then inserted around the base of the penis in order to trap the blood in the penis. With this type of erection, the man is able to achieve vaginal penetration and have intercourse. The device is usually obtained by getting a prescription from a urologist.

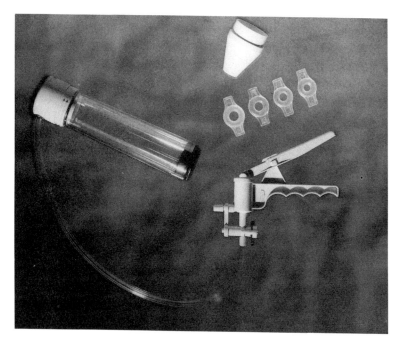

Figure 4. Piston vacuum erection system (courtesy of Mentor Urology).

16 How do I use a vacuum device when I have limited use of my hands?

Many men who have limited use of their hands have their partner learn to use the device. This can be taught by the nurse or the doctor. Another option is for the man with the spinal cord injury to instruct his partner at home after he has been trained in the doctor's office. Since there are few complications, this is generally very safe and has worked well for many couples. The techniques are not complicated but must be followed carefully. Using this device should be avoided if the couple have consumed alcohol or other drugs.

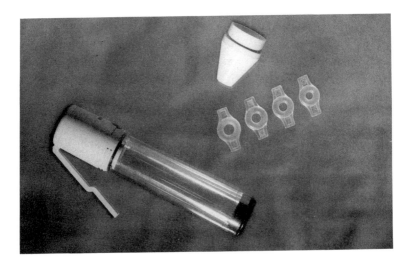

Figure 5. Response battery-powered vacuum erection system (courtesy of Mentor Urology).

17 Are most men satisfied using a vacuum device?

Most men with spinal cord injuries can achieve a rigid erection suitable for vaginal penetration using the vacuum device. This may even be true for men who have penile implants. Studies have shown that up to 80% of men find the vacuum device satisfying and continue to use it for a prolonged period of time. These studies have shown improvements in self-esteem and a sense of well-being. The complaints about the device seem to center on the interruption of sexual activity that is necessary in order to use it. Men have also complained that the device does not feel natural and that it makes the sex act seem mechanical and overly clinical. In many parts of the United States, however, this device is the preferred treatment for erection problems and has been well received by men and their partners.

18 Can there be complications from using a vacuum device?

No serious injuries have been reported using these devices. Most problems have been minor and have not required treatment by a doctor. You may notice some changes of color and the temperature of the penis, but this is generally normal. But never leave the device on for more than 30 minutes, and be sure that the vacuum is from a reputable manufacturer. Be especially careful if you use products that you find in the back of a magazine or in a local sex shop. No studies have been reported that indicate how often a person can use one of these devices. But one study did show that a man with paraplegia developed skin problems after using the device three times a day for a period of a few days. As always, use moderation and good judgment.

19 Can I still use a vacuum device if I have had an implant in the past or if I use an injection program?

Yes, many men with implants—whether or not they still work—are able to use the vacuum device for their erections. Likewise, vacuums can be used in conjunction with an injection program to improve the quality of erections. There are some special considerations that you need to take to ensure that you do not damage the penis. Check with your urologist before making any changes that could affect your physical well-being.

20 What types of penile implants are available?

All penile implants are surgically inserted under the skin and fill the cavernous spaces of the penis. These are the spaces that the blood would fill if the man were getting an erection. Although there are various types of implants, they are generally classified as semi-rigid or inflatable.

The semi-rigid implant is bendable in order to conceal the erection when the man is not having sex. It still may tend to move around, and some men find it embarrassing when others notice the erection. Other semi-rigid implants have several joints that can bend into a functional position. Erections with these types of devices are very reliable and work well for intercourse.

The inflatable implant is inflated when the man is ready to have sex and is deflated at all other times. Many men find this device more natural, as it cannot be noticed when the

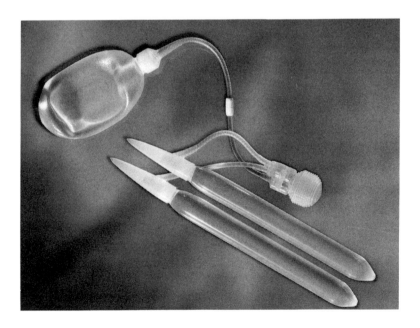

Figure 6.   Alpha I inflatable penile implant (courtesy of Mentor Urology).

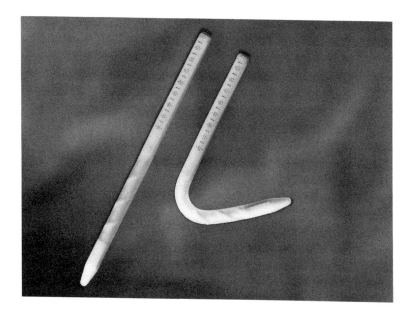

Figure 7. Acu-form bendable penile implant (courtesy of Mentor Urology).

man is not sexually active. The implant is put into each side of the shaft of the penis, with a reservoir inserted into the abdomen of the man. When he is ready for sex, he simply pumps a small bulb in the scrotum, and the fluid fills the chambers in the penis. After sex, squeezing the bulb allows the fluid to return to the reservoir and deflates the erection. Men with limited hand use may find it necessary to have their partner assist them in pumping up the erection. Many couples do this anyway as part of their foreplay before intercourse.

21 Should I get a penile implant?

That decision is a very serious decision, and one that only you can make, with input from your partner. It is a decision that most urologists suggest be made no sooner than 6 months to a year after injury, when you've had a chance to be sexually active again.

One of the most common mistakes that men make is thinking that an implant will restore feelings of potency they had prior to the injury. Men who make the decision based on these hopes are usually very disappointed. The implant will make the penis erect again for intercourse. It won't bring back what you've lost. The erect penis may not look like it did before your accident. It may be shorter; it may be thinner. Also, certain parts of the penis may seem larger than others. You or your partner may initially feel turned off when you inflate the prosthesis. All of these changes require time and adjustments. It may take months after the surgery to even feel like having sex again.

For many couples, however, an implant is a very positive step and adds much enjoyment to their sexual life. If you consider having an implant, examine your reasons. Are you trying to hold on to a partner or to an old image of yourself? Will a prosthesis achieve the desired results, or are you hoping for more than what is realistically possible with the surgery? Once you and your partner are clear about your motives, get as much information as possible; talk to other men who have had an implant after an injury of this nature.

22 Are implants permanent?

Implants should generally be considered permanent. Although they can be removed if problems such as infection occur, implants can cause serious damage to the chambers or spongy tissue of the penis. As a result, other treatments such as injections may not be effective after an implant. (Men with implants, however, can often still use vacuum devices, even with the implant in place.)

Implant surgery is a serious decision and should be considered a last resort. Many urologists recommend trying a vacuum device or injection therapy before an implant. If there was trauma to the penis at the time of your spinal cord injury, the implant may be the best solution because of leakage in the veins of the penis. If you have any doubts, consult several doctors. Also, it may be helpful to speak with another man who has had an implant to learn firsthand of the pros and cons.

23 What kind of side effects can develop from an implant?

Implants have improved a great deal since the mid-1980s. In the past, some devices broke in the flexible joints of the semi-rigid rods or other mechanical problems arose. These days the chances of mechanical failure are relatively slim. Another problem is rejection by the body because of infection. Again, most infections have been eliminated, and today approximately 95% of implant surgeries are said to be effective. A word of caution, however. A certain amount of time is necessary for adjustment after an implant. Most men believe that an implant will give them the erections they had before their injury. This probably will not be the case. The erections are generally different after the implant and will require practice and time to achieve a level of comfort.

24 What is papaverine?

Papaverine hydrocloride is a vasodilator that is often mixed with other drugs such as Regitine (phentobmine mesylate USP) and prostaglandin. It is then injected into one of the chambers of the penis to create an erection. Today, thousands of men throughout the United States inject themselves or have their partner inject them when they wish to engage in sexual activities. With proper training and careful administration, side effects are minimal or nonexistent.

25 Will a penile injection program allow me to have a climax and ejaculation?

No, injection programs can improve only your erections. They will have no impact on your ability to climax and ejaculate. These are separate physical mechanisms and have nothing to do with each other. Some doctors, however, have found that using a vibrator on the shaft of the penis may cause an ejaculation. This may be true regardless of the length of time since injury. This method has been used as a way of obtaining sperm for couples who would like to have a child. It is important to remember that each spinal cord

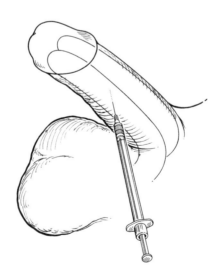

Figure 8.   Penile injection system.

injury is very different, and what works for one person may or may not work for the next person.

26 Are there side effects from using a penile injection program?

Any good injection program generally provides education and training on how to safely inject the penis in order to get an erection. The secrets of using this technique are applying pressure on the injection site for up to 5 minutes after injection (or the time period indicated by your urologist) and using only the prescribed medication. Do not use any more than your urologist has prescribed. Some men have reported scarring of the penis with frequent injections, but this can usually be avoided with the proper technique. Priapism is another possible side effect. This happens when the erection does not go down until 1 or 2 hours after injection. If the erection persists, you should call your urologist or go to an emergency room where medication can be given to bring down the erection.

27 Is there surgery that can improve my erections?

There are no surgical procedures to improve erections after neurological damage, as the primary problem involves neural regulation rather than blood flow. Some men without spinal cord injury may be candidates for vascular bypass operations. These may be men who have experienced a trauma to the pelvic region or men whose penile arteries have become blocked and are functioning poorly. Generally, surgical procedures are rare these days because overall success rates are poor. These procedures also tend to be very expensive and are only done in a few large medical centers.

In addition to vascular surgery, penile implants are available and are inserted by an operation on the penis. Although they will provide an erection, the implant does not repair your body's own ability to have an erection.

28   Is it normal to have erection problems as you get older?

The normal consequences of aging will affect the quality of your erections. However, impotence is not something that typically happens as men get older. Generally, it takes more work to maintain an erection as you get older, and the erection may not be as hard as it was when you were younger. Emotional factors and medical conditions may also affect your erections as you get older. If you are able to have an ejaculation, the time between ejaculations may be also longer as age increases.

For men with spinal cord injuries, these factors will also play a role in the quality of your erections just as they would if you had never been injured. Perhaps you were able to get erections in the early years after your injury, but as you became older this became increasingly more difficult. Should erections change during the years since your injury, you may want to see a urologist for a reevaluation. There may be treatments that can restore the erections you once enjoyed.

29   How important is penis size?

This is an age-old question. We men place a lot of value on a large penis and feel that it is a reflection of our masculinity

and strength. Women tend not to be so concerned about penis size, and studies have shown that they are more attracted
to a man who is sensitive, caring, and warm. There probably
is much truth to the old saying "It's not what you have but
how you use it that counts."

If you are concerned about the size or looks of your penis, ask your partner or someone else about it. Get some
feedback and see how others perceive your penis or any part
of your body. This might help to reduce anxiety and to make
you feel more comfortable with your own body. Every partner has different feelings as to the importance of penis size,
and the only way to answer this question is to bring up the
topic. (Good luck.)

30 Is masturbation normal?

Masturbation is not only normal—most people masturbate
throughout their lives. It is a wonderful way to learn about
your body, your sexual responses, and what gives you pleasure. There is nothing physically or psychologically wrong
about masturbation. In our society, however, some people
believe masturbation is abnormal and look down on it. You
have to decide your own views and values about masturbation. Then you can determine if masturbation is an option
for yourself.

31 Can I masturbate after injury?

You should be able to masturbate safely whenever you have
the privacy and the desire to do so. Your doctor will inform

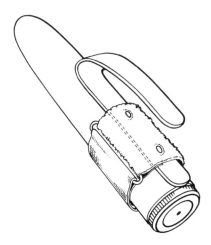

Figure 9.   Vibrator adapted for an individual with limited hand use.

you when your spine has become stable and there is no danger of hurting yourself. If you have a halo in place, it will protect your spinal column so that there is no danger of additional injury. It is generally a good idea to explore your body shortly after injury and find out where and how you can experience pleasure. If you can't use your hands, consider using a vibrator or asking a partner to assist you. Don't limit yourself to your genital areas. Other parts of your body may be more sensitive now and may feel very erotic when touched. Be creative and imaginative in exploring how you can give yourself sexual pleasure. It is a natural and healthy activity that you can enjoy when you are ready to do so.

32   Can I hurt myself if I masturbate too much?

No, you cannot hurt yourself by masturbating too much. However, if you use a vibrator, be careful of sudden changes in your blood pressure (dysreflexia). Masturbation becomes a concern only if you are doing it so often that you are missing out on social opportunities and if it keeps you from doing other things that you may want to be doing. Sometimes it may seem easier to masturbate rather than to go out and try to meet a partner. As a result, you could become isolated and fearful of new situations. Of course, masturbation should be done in private so that it does not offend other people. In general, masturbation is a healthy way to learn about your body and how it functions after a spinal cord injury.

33 Is there anything wrong with using a vibrator?

There is nothing abnormal about using a vibrator for stimulation. Vibrators produce a focused and intense sensation that many people find very pleasurable. There still are some myths about vibrators, for instance that they are addictive, that women who use them are perverted, or that using them will make you less interested in a partner. There is no truth to these myths. Even so, many people have fears about the use of sexual devices or toys. It is useful to understand these fears and make choices based on your own values and interests rather than on myths.

34 Do men ever use vibrators?

There is nothing wrong with a man using a vibrator. Vibrators can be a source of great pleasure for either gender, and couples often will give and receive pleasure by using them.

Vibrators can be very pleasurable on parts of the body where there is limited sensation or on parts not usually considered to be sexual organs. For example, many men find pleasure using a vibrator on the nipples, chest, and neck. Both genders find it pleasurable to use a vibrator in the genital and anal areas. Using a vibrator on the penis may trigger an ejaculation for men with injuries above T12. When using a vibrator, however, you should watch for any signs of autonomic dysreflexia (a sudden, drastic increase in blood pressure, usually brought on by stimulation, which can be life-threatening), such as redness on the skin, increased heart rate, or high blood pressure.

35 Is it dangerous to use a vibrator?

Using a vibrator can be a positive and healthy way to enjoy your sexuality—with or without a partner. It is not dangerous if the vibrator is clean and you have sufficient natural or artificial lubrication. However, be careful of dysreflexia when using the vibrator. Stop if you begin to feel dizzy or lightheaded or if your heart begins to pound harder in your chest.

36 Do women have fantasies? About what? What about wet dreams?

Women certainly do have sexual fantasies. Many of us may have been taught that sexual thoughts were wrong, but it is normal and natural to fantasize. Fantasizing about sexual activity or about a person does not necessarily lead to doing what you were thinking about. Many women imagine sexual activities they would not actually choose to do. The variety of women's sexual fantasies is as large as the variety of human sexual behavior. Fantasies may include memories of past sexual experiences, as well as things that you've read about or seen on film, heard about, or imagined. Women also experience sexual dreams that can produce orgasms during sleep. These are called "wet dreams," a term that usually refers to the nocturnal emissions of sperm for men but that can also refer to the night-time lubrication of a woman's vagina. You may or may not recall the dream in the morning or be aware of the arousal or the orgasm that you experienced during the night. Once again, though, this is normal and not necessarily a sign that you are frustrated in your sex life or "oversexed" in general.

37 How can a woman masturbate?

Touching and stroking the entire body can help a woman identify the places that arouse her. Many women focus on the breasts, nipples, and vulva, including the vaginal lips, the clitoris, and surrounding areas. Some women find pleasure in inserting a finger or dildo in the vagina. There are alternatives to manual stimulation. Some women direct a stream of water on the vulva. Vibrators can also intensify the erotic response. Vibrators can also relax the muscle tension throughout the body.

38 Do I still become lubricated after a spinal cord injury?

Lubrication depends on the level and completeness of your spinal cord injury. You may find that lubrication may be reduced or absent during sexual excitement. If you want to keep the vagina moist for insertion of the penis (or fingers or sex toys), use an artificial, water-soluble lubricant. It will help to prevent uncomfortable friction and possible infection.

Even if you find that you have little or no lubrication and sensation in the vagina, most women after a spinal cord injury retain enough responsiveness to produce an orgasm and rhythmic contractions of genital organs after sexual stimulation. These changes in the body also can induce a strong psychological reaction. It is common for women to experience any number of emotional reactions to changes in lubrication and sensation. If you experience feelings of loss, depression, or inadequacy, discuss these feelings with someone close to you, or a peer counselor, who can offer suggestions.

39 Where is my clitoris?

Your clitoris is an area rich in sensory nerves, located where your inner vaginal lips, or labia, meet. The vaginal lips form a hood over the rounded head of the clitoris. During intercourse, the movement of the labia over the clitoris produces feelings of pleasure. The penis doesn't actually touch the clitoris directly, but the thrusting of the penis into the vagina causes the lips to rub on the clitoris. Additional stimulation during intercourse, or as an alternative to it, can be achieved by rubbing near or on the clitoris. Some women find the clitoris too sensitive to be touched directly and find it more pleasurable to be touched in the areas close to the clitoris instead. The sensation caused by clitoral stimulation depends on your level of injury. Early after injury, it is a good idea to experiment and see what types of stimulation feel the most pleasurable to you. After your injury, you may also find that other parts of your body have become increasingly sensitive and provide you with sexual pleasure in a way that was not possible before.

40 What is my G spot?

The G spot is an area of tissue on the front wall of the vagina. On a small number of women, stimulation of this area produces an intense orgasmic response accompanied by a gush of fluid. While the source of this "female ejaculate" is a matter of debate, it is not simply a leakage of urine. The research that originally described this phenomenon, however, still awaits verification.

41 Will I ever have an orgasm again?

This is a difficult question that really can't be answered in a general way. There are many factors involved, especially the level of your spinal cord injury. Also, time may play a role. Some men and women report that orgasm has returned months or years after injury.

Some men talk about a psychological orgasm that is compared to a "rush" or "high" experience. This may be a combination of fantasy, memories of orgasms, and the excitement of the whole sexual experience. With time, some men report that this type of experience can get better as the couple relaxes and becomes more comfortable with each other. Experimentation is the key here, and each man will experience different pleasurable sensations during sex. Try to broaden the types of good feelings associated with sexual pleasure. Get in touch with the various changes that take place in your body and your partner's as the two of you become sexually excited. Some of these sensations can become pleasurable, and parts of your body may become more sensitive and sensual when they are touched in a sexual way.

Likewise, some women have reported what they call a "para-orgasm." This means that the orgasm they experience is different from genital orgasm and has a unique quality to it. It may be a combination of physical sensation, emotional responses, memories, fantasies, and visual/auditory stimulation, and more of a whole-body response than vaginal contractions or clitoral throbbing. It is not lesser or greater than a genital orgasm, just different. It is important to explore your own body and to determine and enjoy the kind of response that you are able to achieve.

If you do experience a type of para-orgasm and if your injury is above the T6 level, you may need to be concerned about quick changes in your blood pressure, known as hyperreflexia. Should this occur, discontinue the sexual stimulation and speak to your doctor about possible solutions to the problem.

If you have reduced sensation in your body, consider alternatives that may enhance the nonphysical aspects of your sexual pleasure. For example, have your partner describe his or her fantasies, leave the lights on, play sensual music, and enjoy your own fantasy life. These suggestions can add to your pleasure and help build a sense of sexual excitement. For some people, they can be just as pleasurable as a physical orgasm.

42 What is an emotional orgasm?

Orgasms are a complex brew of physical and emotional sensations. On the physical level, you will typically experience an intense sensation of pleasure followed by a release in the form of an ejaculation of semen from your urethra (the tube inside your penis) for men or by genital throbbing for women. After a spinal cord injury, these sensations may be altered or absent, but the emotional components of an orgasm are still intact and they can be just as rewarding and fulfilling. With practice and an increased understanding of your body, you can reach a peak of sexual experience sometimes known as an "emotional orgasm."

This release is achieved by visual, auditory, and tactile stimulation of your body and your partner's. Memories, sexual fantasies, and feelings of closeness service to enhance the experience. Sex talk—or "talking dirty"—can also add to your excitement. The important thing is to be creative and experiment with various ways of giving and receiving pleasure. As you do, monitor the changes in your body and work on bringing those sensations to a peak and a release.

43 Can I come more than once?

Possibly. Women are capable of being re-aroused immediately if the proper stimulation is continued. Some women are regularly multiorgasmic, while others will only have one orgasm. All of these are normal responses. Some women may choose to engage in sexual growth programs, through self-help or therapy, to expand the circumstances that help them experience orgasm. Some women are more readily orgasmic with some partners than others. Other women are more responsive as their relationship with their partner grows and deepens. In summary, your ability to have an orgasm may change over time and in various relationships.

Men generally have a period of time when they cannot be re-aroused after orgasm. During this refractory period, another ejaculation may not be possible even if the man can

achieve another erection. The length of this period will vary
with age and can range from about 10 minutes for young
men to about 45 minutes in older ones. If you are able to
achieve an ejaculation after your spinal cord injury, the time
between ejaculations may be quite long. Some men have reported that they are able to achieve an ejaculation only once
per day. If your orgasms are more emotional and feel like a
"rush" experience, you may also have a refractory period
between these experiences. These are very individual responses, however, and the best way to learn about your
body is through experimentation and practice.

44 Why do I have an erection but don't ejaculate?

The mechanisms of erection and ejaculation are totally separate functions. Men with upper motor neuron lesions (quadriplegics) can generally have reflex erections, but have difficulty sustaining them during sexual intercourse. Other men
can ejaculate, but are unable to sustain an erection; they ejaculate with a flaccid penis and often do not feel the pleasurable sensations that we associate with climax. There is no
way to determine the degree of your sexual functioning because it depends on the damage done to the various nerves
of the spinal cord.

45 How do I explain my bladder and bowel to a new partner?

Talking about sex with a potential partner is something that
everyone should do, regardless of whether or not they have
a spinal cord injury. Talking about sex could, for example,

greatly reduce the numbers of unwanted pregnancies and cases of sexually transmitted diseases. Your sexual encounter can be even more romantic if you are not worrying about incontinence. Explain briefly what your bladder and bowel requirements are, that you prepare for sex by voiding and emptying your bowels, that you like to put protective pads under you, how to clean up if an unlikely accident occurs, and how you feel about all of this. Ask how your partner feels as well. There is nothing intrinsically horrible about urine or feces. They may not be pleasant, but they are hardly deadly either. If an accident occurs, you can respond in a matter-of-fact manner if you have dealt with your attitudes beforehand. Keeping a sense of humor is often helpful in areas that can be anxiety provoking.

46 Should I have sex when I have a bladder infection?

Maintaining a regular bladder program and good hygiene is helpful in preventing infections. If you get one, see your doctor for a program of antibiotics to treat the infection. Prevention strategies include drinking lots of water to keep the bladder flushed, voiding completely (or catheterizing as needed), and washing the vulva often. In addition, wearing loose cotton underwear, changing sanitary pads frequently, and following a low-acid diet (including daily yogurt) will help to prevent infections. Avoid using bubble baths, vaginal sprays, and douches as much as possible. Finally, make sure that catheters are sterile and that catheterizations are done so that bacteria are not introduced into your body.

It is best not to have sexual intercourse or oral sex while you have a urinary tract infection. Sexual activity may make the infection worse, and it is possible to pass it to your partner. Instead, wait until the infection clears and wash your genitals on a regular and frequent basis.

47 What do I do with my leg bag?

If you're in bed, it's best to remove the leg bag and use a drainage bag attached to the side of the bed. If you're having sex on a couch or in a chair, it's alright to keep the leg bag on, but make sure it is emptied and out of the way. Also, secure it in a position where it won't be pulled and it won't interfere with your movements or your partner's. Accidents, however, will happen, and when they do it's better to have a funny line handy to defuse the embarrassment than to sulk or turn off. Keep in mind that humor, too, can be a great aphrodisiac.

48 What if I urinate during sex?

It is possible that you may have a bladder accident during sexual activity. For this reason, you will want to empty your bladder beforehand and reduce your fluid intake before you have sex. You might also want to prepare for an accident by having a towel or a urinal close by. Because we have such strong feelings about bladder and bowel functions, they can be sources of great anxiety and tension after a spinal cord injury. Try to reduce this worry by letting your partner know that an accident may happen. If you do have one, clean up, talk about it, and keep on going.

49 Can I have sex with a catheter in place?

It is possible for men to have sex with the catheter in place, but it depends on the type of system that you use. Some men remove the catheter before sex and then re-insert it when they are finished. Other men fold it down the side of the penis and insert a condom over the penis and the catheter. Intercourse or other types of sexual activity are then possible.

Women can have intercourse with a catheter in place as long as it is taped to the abdomen. Surgical or bandage tape is usually best. This procedure is typically used with indwelling catheters, suprapubic tubes, or ileal loop drainage. If you or your partner feels uncomfortable leaving the catheter in place, a foley catheter may be removed for up to 4 hours. This should allow ample time for preparation, sexual activity, and "afterplay" before the catheter needs to be replaced.

If you are with a new partner, give some thought beforehand about how you will discuss the catheter and leg bag. Some men give their partners the choice of leaving while it is being removed. This an issue that should be discussed before you become intimate. Keep the surprises to a minimum, and give your partner lots of choices about what feels comfortable.

50 Can I have sex with a suprapubic tube in place?

Suprapubic tubes do not create specific difficulties in sexual activity since they are located away from the genital area. It is a good idea, however, to secure them with tape to the body to avoid any unnecessary pulling. More often, suprapubic tubes are a source of anxiety and embarrassment, and there may be feelings of shame in showing the tube to your partner. Feelings such as these are normal and can be best dealt with by straightforward communication and experimentation. Many people believe that showing the tube to a partner is best done during nonsexual times. This gives the partner a chance to adjust to the tube during a less stressful time.

51 Can I minimize the chance of bowel accident?

The fear of bowel accidents is naturally a major concern for most people after a spinal cord injury. If you are on a regular bladder/bowel management program, however, there is no reason to expect that sexual activity will put you off schedule or cause an accident. Time, however, is a factor that you have some control over. Eating or drinking just before sexual activity may increase the chances of an accident. In the same way, there is less of a chance of an accident if your bladder and bowel have been emptied prior to your sexual activity. The most important thing is to communicate your anxiety to your partner and be prepared just in case. Have a towel handy. If your partner knows of your concerns, however, that may decrease your apprehension and improve your overall sexual pleasure.

52 What if I have a bowel movement during sex?

This possibility always exists, but you can take many precautions to minimize the chances of having an accident. Prevention involves a good bowel program and a regular routine. You might want to have a towel and absorbent pads under you during sex to make clean-up easier. If your problem is passages of gas, you might try various positions or gentler thrusting to minimize this possibility. As always, communication is the most important thing to remember. Talk about this before becoming intimate, and explain why this may occur. Should you have an accident, give your partner clear instructions how to clean up the bed and both of you. As embarrassing as this may be, a little humor can ease the tension and the anxiety that both of you feel.

53 Is there any way that I can increase the pleasure of being touched if I don't have sensation in my body?

To increase the pleasurable sensations of being touched on any part of your body, try to use as many senses as possible. For example, leave the lights on so you can watch your partner touching you and have him or her describe the sensations. Another possibility that some people have found helpful is to put your hand on top of your partner's hand as he or she touches you. By doing this, you may be able to experience the sensations of being touched as your partner touches you.

54 How can I get pleasure when I can't feel in my vagina?

Stimulation of your whole body, even the parts that you cannot feel, contributes to your sexual pleasure. It can stimulate your emotions, your fantasies, and your feelings of closeness to your partner. Also, your senses can be stimulated above the level of injury, often in enhanced ways. Being kissed and caressed on your face, head, shoulders, nipples, and arms may produce intense arousal. (Some people also find that using a vibrator on these parts of the body adds to their pleasure.) But don't neglect areas of reduced or diminished sensation either. Even though you may not have physical sensation in these parts of your body, it can be exciting to see your partner touching you there. It may stir up memories, fantasies, and sexual thoughts that add to the pleasure. Giving pleasure to your partner is another turn-on. Use your mouth and hands, if possible, to pinch, suck, kiss, tickle, rub, and caress your lover. Use your sense of taste, smell, hearing, and sight to add sexual pleasures in ways that you may not have thought of before your injury. Use your imagination and go wild.

55   My skin feels hypersensitive sometimes. What should I do?

Some conditions, such as spinal muscular atrophy, can cause hypersensitivity in certain parts of the body. As a result, it may be painful to be touched on these parts of your body. Usually, however, being touched lightly with your partner's hand or with an object like a feather can be pleasurable. Your partner may be anxious about causing you pain and will look to you for guidance as to what feels pleasurable and enjoyable. Discuss your feelings with your partner and explore your body to find how you can get (and give) pleasure to one another.

56   Pain interferes with my sexual desire. What can I do?

Plan sexual activity for times when your pain is minimal. This may be after you have taken pain medication and have used pain management practices, such as hot packs or relaxation techniques. Make sure that your positions are comfortable and do not intensify your pain. For example, it may be beneficial to make love on a firm surface with your back and neck in alignment. Reduce the force of pelvic thrusting by asking your partner to take it slow and gentle. If pain is persistent, you may need more aggressive medical intervention (nerve blocks, dorsal root rhizotomy [a surgical procedure in which nerves in the spinal cord are severed to reduce pain or spasticity], etc.) to reduce the pain to manageable levels. For some people, a comprehensive pain management program can ultimately lead to a more pleasurable sex life. For others, sexual activity itself has an analgesic affect and can reduce pain levels during or after sex.

57   How can I be sexually active if I am in pain?

Chronic pain after a spinal cord injury does occur with some people, and it can be a source of great stress and frustration. Although specific recommendations may be made by your doctor regarding precautions, the usual approach is to encourage movement and action. Chronic pain tends to increase when muscles are not kept active and are allowed to decondition. You should therefore try to keep moving and remain active despite the discomfort and pain that you are experiencing.

Your pain may also make it difficult for you to express yourself sexually or in other ways. Likewise, your partner may be frightened by your pain and uncertain as to how he or she should approach you. Stretching and warm-up exercises may help you prepare for sexual activity. (Consider doing them with your partner and perhaps incorporating them into your sexual play.) Try to plan sexual activity following periods in which you have been active, such as at the end of the day or after wheeling for considerable distances. Avoid

staying in any one position for too long, and give your partner any information regarding your pain. Avoid sexual activity during periods of heavy fatigue, and experiment with positions that help relieve your pain.

58 Since I can't feel anything, will my partner hurt me during sex?

It's unlikely that you will be hurt during sexual activity, as
long as you are sufficiently lubricated. Have a water-soluble
lubricant handy until you see how well you lubricate naturally after your injury. Also, if your spinal cord injury is high
level, be on the look-out for signs of dysreflexia as you become sexually stimulated. These signs will be flushness of
the skin due to increases in blood pressure. Actually fears
regarding your safety may be more of a concern at first for
your partner. It's common for people to regard a person with
a spinal cord injury as fragile and vulnerable. You may need
to reassure him or her that you are not made of glass and
that you can still enjoy sex together as much as you did before your injury.

59 Will intercourse hurt?

Intercourse should not be painful. If it does hurt, it may be
because there is a lack of natural or artificial lubrication,
causing friction between the walls of the vagina and the penis. If the woman is anxious, tense, or not aroused, the opening of the vagina may also be tight, causing pain when the
penis is inserted. If the woman is a virgin, she may also experience some pain and bleeding when the hymen (a small
ring of tissue inside of the vagina) is separated by the penis

during her first intercourse. Some women have a thick hymen or medical problems, such as a hormone imbalance, that may also contribute to painful intercourse, but these conditions tend to be rare. For women with spinal cord injury, however, the most common reason for painful intercourse is a lack of lubrication. This can be handled quite easily by a water-soluble lubricant placed on the man's penis.

60 What if I have spasms during sex?

Spasms are uncontrolled muscle movements or tremors that can occur in any part of the body. They can be caused by any number of stimuli or may seem totally unpredictable. At times, the excitement of sexual stimulation may also set off spasms in your body. For many people with spinal cord injury, leg or arm spasms are common and happen on a very regular basis.

Having a spasm during sex does not have to be a negative experience, unless it causes discomfort, embarrassment, or pain. It's also a good idea to make your partner aware that a spasm may occur. Should a spasm strike a limb, you may want to put weight on it. You may also want your partner to put weight on the particular leg or arm. Changing positions may also eliminate the spasm. Some people try to use the spasms to enhance their sexual pleasure. For example, placing the area of the spasm on the clitoris may provide your partner with pleasure. If the spasms continue or increase with sexual stimulation, you may want to consult your doctor.

Spasms can be embarrassing for some men. They can also create problems in positioning. It's a good idea to tell your partner about the possibility of having spasms before the two of you become intimate. Some couples will push gently on the legs during a spasm to reduce them or use medication to help control them. But don't assume that spasms are necessarily bad unless you find them painful and uncomfortable. Spasms may actually improve your erections and create movements, like thrusting, that can improve the pleasure both of you get from sex.

61 How do I get ready for sex?

Having sex may require planning and preparation. First of all, you may need to explain how things work to your partner, so that he or she will know what to expect and can be helpful. Try to avoid surprises since they will add tension and make you and your partner uncomfortable. Before starting, think about the kinds of help you may need. Do you need assistance with transferring, getting undressed, or emptying a leg bag? Do you want your partner to leave when you catheterize yourself and empty your bladder? Do you need assistance getting into the right position? Try to be open with your partner and put him or her at ease. The first time for each of you may require learning and experimentation. Take it easy on yourself. Try to relax and enjoy the experience. Assume that things may not go perfectly, and keep your sense of humor. Try not to let your ego get too caught up in the whole experience.

62 How can I reduce the anxiety before sex?

Planning helps make sexual activity more enjoyable and can remove some of the anxiety associated with being intimate. First, choose a time that seems best for you and your partner. Try to find time and a place where you won't be disturbed or rushed. If possible, avoid times when you may be too tired to enjoy the experience. If this is one of the first times that you've been intimate with this partner, choose a time when there is ample opportunity to talk, discuss your concerns, and inform your partner about how your body works. Discuss the kinds of assistance you may require. You will want to have completed your bowel program, voided your bladder (or taped the catheter out of the way), and found a position that seems comfortable. It's a good idea also to have a towel handy in case there is a bladder or bowel accident. Give some thought to the setting as well. Would music, a glass of wine, and romantic lighting enhance the experience for the two of you?

63 Where can I have sex now?

There is no limit to the number of places that people choose to have sex. That doesn't change after a spinal cord injury, although you may need to give a little more thought to what is practical and realistic. Generally, you can have sex wherever you feel comfortable and can have some privacy. Many people like to change the places they have sex and find it exciting to add variety to their lovemaking by being creative in this aspect of sexuality. Talk about it with your partner and have some fun being daring.

64 Can I have sex in my wheelchair?

Having sex in your wheelchair can be fun and different. First, remember to lock the wheels to avoid accidents. Also, remove the arms to give the two of you extra room to maneuver. Your partner may want to sit facing you while both of you make love in a sitting position. You may need to position your legs over your partner's legs in order to ensure maximum genital contact. Your partner may also need to be strong enough to sit upright with his or her arms in order not to squish your legs. Experiment with positions that are fulfilling, comfortable, and safe.

65 How will my partner transfer me into bed?

A transfer is much easier than it may appear. It does not take a great deal of strength or muscle power. Your responsibility is to teach your partner the easiest and safest method to perform the task. If you are still in a rehabilitation program, the physical therapist will be happy to teach any people you feel should know the procedure. If you have been discharged, you should be able to instruct your partner all by yourself. Discuss it beforehand first, and remember to keep a sense of humor and put your partner at ease. If you have forgotten the best method to do a transfer, call the rehabilitation program for a little refresher. After the first time, it should be no big deal for either of you.

66 I can't use the same sexual positions as before my accident. What positions will work for a woman?

If you have been used to lying on your back during intercourse, this may continue to work well if you use a few pillows to support and position your body. A number of other positions are also possible. You might want to support your upper body on the side of the bed while kneeling. Your partner can then enter you from behind. Many women enjoy lying face down on the bed while their partner enters from behind. Lying on top of your partner may also be possible and allows your partner to hold you during your sexual activity. Lying side by side, either face to face or back to front, is another comfortable way to get your bodies in full contact. Sitting positions (in or out of the wheelchair) might also work for you. Movement can occur from rocking together or by your partner rotating your hips with his or her hands or legs wrapped around you. The important aspect of experimentation is to use your imagination and see what works best for you and your partner. Talk about your preferences and enjoy the opportunities to explore new ways of having and giving pleasure to one another.

67 What positions work best for a man?

The most pleasurable positions will depend on your sexual preference and the degree of mobility that you are now able to achieve. Most men with limited mobility find that being on the bottom provides the greatest sense of movement and freedom. Other men find that entering their partner's vagina from the rear in a side-to-side position works very well. Like other aspects of sexuality, this is an individual decision and requires experimentation and practice. When it comes to positions, there is no right or wrong. Try a variety of them and find what works best for you.

68 Can I still be on top during sex?

For many men, being on top during sexual intercourse is very important. It is a position of control, independence, and power. After a spinal cord injury, however, this position may not be as pleasurable for you and will require an extraordinary amount of energy. Most men feel that it is not worth the energy. Try to relax, talk with your partner, and see what new positions the two of you can discover as fun ways of giving and receiving pleasure to each other.

69 Is there a right way to have intercourse?

There is no correct way to have intercourse, and there is no way that is best for everyone. Unfortunately, most people get their sex education from the streets or from movies. As a result, they develop confusion as to what is normal and what they "should be doing." In general, whatever is satisfying and mutually agreeable for the couple is best. There are many positions in which the penis can be placed in the vagina. The most common are with the man on top of a woman lying on her back; the woman sitting or lying on top of the man; the man entering the woman from behind; and both partners facing each other lying on their sides. Each position has advantages in terms of comfort, convenience, and type of stimulation. Some people try them all and change frequently during lovemaking. Others use only one.

Your level of injury and mobility will make a big difference in determining the position that works best for you. If balance is a problem and you have limitations in your movement, it may be best to lie on your back so that your partner can be more active. Lying on your side with your partner behind you may also work well. If you have some sensation, the position you choose will also depend on where you are able to feel the maximum stimulation. Experiment and learn what pleases you and your partner.

4
Fertility, Feminine Hygiene, and Parenting

1. What are the chances of getting a woman pregnant?

2. Why is fertility such a big problem for men with spinal cord injury?

3. Is there anything that I can do to improve the chances of fathering a child?

4. What is vibratory stimulation?

5. What is electroejaculation?

6. What is a sperm bank, and should men with spinal cord injury bank their sperm there?

7. Are birth control pills dangerous?

8. What's the best kind of birth control for women?

9. How do I put in a diaphragm?

10. How can I get help in handling PMS?

11. When will I get my period again?

12. My period is late. Am I pregnant?

13. How can I keep myself clean and fresh during my period?

14. Can menstrual pads cause skin breakdowns?

15. Will tampons hurt me? What if they get stuck inside me?

16. How do I know if I need to douche?

17. What is normal vaginal discharge?

18. Do I still need a pelvic exam each year?

19. Can I still have children?

20. Can I adopt a child now that I have a spinal cord injury?

21. When should I consider genetic counseling?

22. What would it be like to be pregnant with a spinal cord injury?

23. Can I get pregnant from anal sex?

24. How do I know if I am in labor if I can't feel my body?

25. Can I still breast-feed my baby after a spinal cord injury?

26. Can I be a good mother?

27. How can I be a father in a wheelchair?

28. Can my kids adjust to me being in a wheelchair?

1 What are the chances of getting a woman pregnant?

Doctors used to think that men had a 90% infertility rate after spinal cord injury. Today, urologists have learned that many men have viable sperm years after injury. Once the semen has been obtained, artificial insemination has allowed many men with spinal cord injury to father children and enjoy the rewards of parenthood. New fertility drugs for women, along with artificial insemination, have also enhanced the odds. No one can definitely say if you can father a child, but you should find a urologist who specializes in fertility for men with spinal cord injury.

2 Why is fertility such a big problem for men with spinal cord injury?

The fertility problem for men with spinal cord injuries is twofold. First, the inability of the man to ejaculate creates difficulties in the sperm reaching the uterus of the woman. Second, it has long been felt (although no evidence seems to exist) that men with spinal cord injuries have poor quality sperm with low motility. In recent years, cases of men impregnating their wives many years after the injury have seriously challenged this theory. Today we know that each man is different. Some retain the ability to produce sperm, while others seems to develop certain impairments in the testes early after injury that halt the production of semen.

3 Is there anything that I can do to improve the chances of fathering a child?

For many years, it was believed that the quality of sperm production in men with spinal cord injury was low because of increases in scrotal temperatures. Doctors supposed that the mechanism to regulate testicular temperatures was somehow impaired as a result of the injury. As a result, they recommended that men keep their knees apart when sitting, wear underwear with a scrotal slit, and prop the scrotum onto the thighs whenever possible. There was never any research to support these suppositions, and even today the mechanisms of sperm production in men with spinal cord injury are little understood. Nevertheless, some doctors continue to believe that actions such as these will make a difference in sperm quality and quantity.

4 What is vibratory stimulation?

Vibratory stimulation was originally developed by an English physician named G.S. Brindley. It involves placing a vibrator on the underside of the glans penis in order to achieve emission and ejaculation. The use of the vibrator causes a reflex mechanism that in many cases allows the man to ejaculate. It is generally only successful in men with lesions above T12, since the thoracic and sacral areas must be intact. Under medical supervision, the man can use this procedure at home and the sperm can be artificially inseminated, by a physician, into the woman's uterus. Studies indicate that between 50% and 70% of men with injuries above T12 are successful in achieving ejaculation when using this technique. Autonomic dysreflexia is a major complication of this procedure, but can be controlled with medication.

5 What is electroejaculation?

Electroejaculation is gaining popularity in the United States as a way to assist men with spinal cord injuries in fathering children. The procedure involves placing an electrode in the rectum of the man and electrically stimulating the prostate and seminal vesicles. This contracts the muscles and produces ejaculation. The procedure is timed with the woman's ovulation so that the semen can be artificially inseminated into her uterus. These techniques result in successful pregnancies about 40% of the time.

6 What is a sperm bank, and should men with spinal cord injury bank their sperm there?

A sperm bank preserves sperm for many years by freezing specimens at very low temperatures. When the man is ready to have a child, the sperm are then warmed and used in artificial insemination or in vitro fertilization. At one time, it was felt that placing a specimen in a sperm bank was a good idea as soon as possible after injury. Samples were even obtained in the emergency room a few hours after an injury. In more recent years, this procedure has virtually stopped, mostly because of the success that urologists and gynecologists are having in improving fertility rates among couples where the man has an injury. Nevertheless, using a sperm bank is an option worth considering if you are thinking of having a child in the future.

7 Are birth control pills dangerous?

New low-dosage birth control pills have many fewer side effects than when the pill was first introduced. Spotting and bleeding between periods are the main side effects women notice. Some physicians, however, have concerns about an increased possibility of blood clots. Because women can develop circulation problems from long stretches of sitting in a wheelchair, they should be checked by their doctors to make sure the pill is not contributing to the risk of blood clots. Blood clots are most common in the first 6 months after injury. As a result, some doctors feel that it is a good idea not to start the pill during this time of your rehabilitation.

Women who smoke have a greater risk of stroke and heart attack when they use birth control pills. This risk increases with age. If you have undetected breast cancer, the pill can make the cancer grow faster. But it also seems as if the pill protects you from cancer of the ovaries and of the lining of the uterus. The longer you take the pill, the more protection it offers you, even after you stop.

In summary, if you are in a committed relationship and want to delay having children, pills are a good choice for many women. If you do not have sex regularly or have several partners, it may be better to choose a method with fewer risks that also affords protection against AIDS, herpes, genital warts, and infections.

8 What's the best kind of birth control for women?

There is no single form of birth control that is best for every woman. There are advantages and disadvantages to each type. However, because of the AIDS epidemic, everyone is encouraged to have safer sex and to use condoms, whether

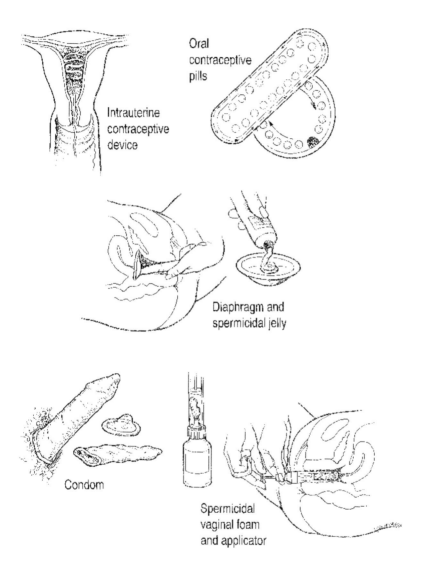

Intrauterine contraceptive device

Oral contraceptive pills

Diaphragm and spermicidal jelly

Condom

Spermicidal vaginal foam and applicator

Figure 10. Birth control options.

as a means of birth control or not. For all women, birth control pills are often regarded as having the highest success rate—about 95% effective. The failures are often associated with improper use of the pill, such as taking it on an irregular schedule and forgetting to take it daily. In the past, women with spinal cord injury were discouraged from using birth control pills because of difficulties in circulation. Today, many physicians believe that the newer pills are safe for women whether they use a wheelchair or not.

Barrier methods of birth control, such as condoms and diaphragms, also have a high success rate, especially when they are used in conjunction with spermicidal foams or gels. The disadvantage of these methods is usually related to interruption of sex in order to put on the condom or insert the diaphragm. A condom should be placed on the penis prior to any sexual activity since it may be difficult to put it on as passion intensifies. In addition, it is possible for the woman to get pregnant from the pre-ejaculate. Although unlikely, it is possible for the pre-ejaculate to penetrate the woman and cause pregnancy prior to intercourse. In a similar manner, diaphragms should be inserted at the beginning of sexual activity since it may be difficult to stop during foreplay. Women with spinal cord injury may also have difficulty inserting the diaphragm because of reduced movement of the hands and fingers. In such cases, the partner can be instructed to insert it as part of the foreplay.

Intrauterine devices (IUDs) have the advantage of being placed by a doctor, but they do not prevent sexually transmitted diseases. Also, women with spinal cord injury may have difficulty detecting the pain associated with serious complications, such as pelvic inflammatory disease or perforation of the uterine wall. Women using the IUD should be checked periodically for iron deficiency often associated with this device.

New implants have been developed that can be inserted in the armpit. These forms of birth control gradually release progestin for up to 5 years, but research has also begun to show that these new forms of birth control have side effects, including menstrual irregularities, headaches, acne, hair loss, and weight gain.

Permanent methods of birth control include tubal ligation for the woman and vasectomy for the man.

With these methods, condoms are still recommended to prevent the spread of sexually transmitted diseases. The female condom is now becoming available. It is under the woman's control (in case her partner refuses the male condom) and protects against disease. What method is best for you? Talk to your doctor, and weigh the risks and benefits of each.

How do I put in a diaphragm?

Your doctor or nurse practitioner can fit you with the proper size diaphragm, instruct you on its use, and check it after you or your partner have practiced inserting it. Begin by filling the cupped portion of the diaphragm with spermicidal foam or gel and spread it along the inner surfaces that come in contact with the cervix. Then squeeze the flexible rim together so it forms an oval shape and slide it into the vagina with the open side facing the front. When it reaches the end of the vagina, release the rim and it will spring into place. Check to feel if it is secure and covering the cervical opening. It shouldn't feel uncomfortable to you and your partner when it is inserted properly.

Some drug stores carry inserters for women with limited hand motion or for those who do not like to put their fingers into the vagina. Take your time and practice several times before having intercourse. If you are teaching a partner, be patient and help with some of the emotional issues that your partner may have inserting it for you. Keep a sense of humor about inserting the diaphragm, and try to put both of you at ease with a little comic relief.

10   How can I get help in handling PMS?

Premenstrual syndrome (PMS) varies widely among women and at present is not well understood by physicians and mental health professionals. You are in good company needing help understanding it, however, since many women find it confusing and troubling. The most frequent symptoms are noted just before or at the end of the menstrual period. The symptoms typically seen are mood changes, such as anxiety, irritability, and depression; physical changes, such as fatigue, headaches, and bloating; and cognitive changes, such as confusion and forgetfulness.

Many women find that healthy changes in diet (low-fat, high-complex carbohydrates), exercise, and stress reduction decrease the severity of their symptoms. Other women, especially those with severe symptoms, may be helped with medications, such as hormones or antidepressant medications. The best person with whom to talk about PMS is your doctor. But you may find that little information is available to help you through these difficult times. You may want to talk with other women or contact your local independent living center.

11   When will I get my period again?

For up to about 6 months following a spinal cord injury, about one out of two women temporarily stops menstruating. The level of the injury does not determine whether your menstrual cycle will stop during the postinjury phase. Menstruation will resume on its own. The length of your menstrual cycle may be different, as may the duration and amount of your blood flow. The intensity and amount of pain may change after the injury too. Although menstrual cycles usually resume after 6 months, the delay ranges from several months to several days.

Although your menstrual cycle may be interrupted, ovulation is not affected by your injury. Therefore, you will still be fertile, and you'll need to keep this in mind when you engage in sexual intercourse.

12 My period is late. Am I pregnant?

It typically takes at least several months after your injury to resume normal menstruation. It can vary from woman to woman, and your cycle may be different from the way it was before your accident. A number of other factors other than pregnancy can cause your period to be late. The normal menstrual cycle often varies between 25 and 35 days. Stress and illness can cause the cycle to fluctuate even more. Losing weight after a spinal cord injury can also delay menstruation. If you have only recently begun to menstruate or if you are nearing menopause, your periods may already be irregular, and the injury will intensify the irregularity.

However, if you suspect that you are pregnant and are missing periods over a long stretch of time, see your doctor to find out what is going on. It will also ease your mind if you are feeling anxious about the possibility of pregnancy. Should you be pregnant, it is a good idea to find out as soon as possible in order to begin healthy prenatal care or make other important decisions regarding your pregnancy.

13 How can I keep myself clean and fresh during my period?

Changing sanitary napkins or tampons frequently should provide you with cleanliness and hygiene that are important for good health. Regularly washing the vulva with un-scented soap and water will also be helpful. Feminine hy-giene sprays and douches often contain chemicals that irri-tate sensitive vagina tissues; however, a douche may be helpful in clearing infections. Find a brand that is sensitive and as natural as possible. If the infection persists, your doc-tor may have some suggestions.

14 Can menstrual pads cause skin breakdowns?

Yes, if you leave them on for too long they will cause irrita-tion on the skin and can eventually lead to a breakdown of the skin's integrity. It is important to change pads and tam-pons frequently to avoid infection and to reduce any possi-bility of damage to the skin. If you have limited use of your arms and hands because of your injury, it will be important to determine how to change pads and tampons both at home and outside. This may involve some adjustment on your part, since it may not be easy to have someone else help with such a personal matter.

15 Will tampons hurt me? What if they get stuck inside me?

Used correctly, tampons usually do not hurt you. A small percentage of women, however, do experience a strong adverse physical reaction, known as toxic shock syndrome. Also, leaving tampons in for too long can increase your chances of infection or toxic shock syndrome.

For proper use, read the package directions for information on how to insert the tampon. If the muscles around the vagina are tight because of spasms or tension, it may be uncomfortable to insert the tampon. A tampon cannot get stuck inside the vagina since it can go in only as far as your cervix. Tampons can usually be reached with your fingers, even if the string comes off. In an emergency, a doctor or partner can remove a tampon for you. If you have limited use of arms, hands, and fingers, you will need to decide how to handle your periods and the changing of tampons or pads. Often, personal care attendants or partners can assist on a regular basis. You might be able to be more independent if you switch from tampons to pads, which can be changed more easily.

16 How do I know if I need to douche?

Under normal circumstances, women don't need to douche at all. In fact, the usual biological balance of the vagina can be upset by douching. The vagina cleans itself, and external hygiene can be maintained by daily washing of the vulva with unscented soap and water. Unless your doctor prescribes douching for a specific purpose, it is unnecessary. Some women like to douche before sexual activity because of natural genital odors that might be regarded as offensive by partners. In such cases, washing the vulva with soap and water before sexual activity should solve the problem.

17 What is normal vaginal discharge?

Vaginal discharge is made of fluid drops produced by the vagina in response to sexual arousal plus mucus that is produced by the cervix at various times during the menstrual cycle. The discharge is usually noticed at the vaginal opening. This normal vaginal discharge occurs in all women. The amount is usually very small, but can vary from woman to woman. The consistency of the fluid may be thick, sticky, and slightly cloudy. It may also have a mild odor. During ovulation, at about the 14th day of a normal 28-day cycle, the consistency changes and becomes clearer and more rubbery. If the discharge increases in volume and becomes yellow or white in color, it may be a sign of vaginal infection, especially if the odor becomes stronger as well. If so, it is usually necessary to see your doctor and get medication.

18 Do I still need a pelvic exam each year?

Yes, your injury does not change the need for good preventive health care on an annual basis. Pelvic and breast exams should be conducted on a regular basis, as they should for all women. Again, the presence of a spinal cord injury does not decrease the chances of health problems. The challenge may be finding the right health professional to provide the examinations or the care that you may require. There are women's health centers that specialize in women's issues, but may not have the expertise in spinal cord injury or may not be wheelchair accessible. There are also rehabilitation centers that do have the expertise in spinal cord injury, but lack awareness of women's health issues. Because of federal legislation (the Americans with Disabilities Act), you have the right to be seen wherever you wish, but you may have to do some homework to ensure that you are getting the quality of care that you deserve.

19 Can I still have children?

Spinal cord injury does not prevent pregnancy, unless you have an unrelated fertility problem. Should that be the case, the possibility of pregnancy is the same as before your injury. Be aware, however, that you may face discrimination by the medical establishment if you decide to have a child. Medical professionals and the community at large may question your judgment, claiming that it will be unfair to the child and that you are not capable of being a good parent. It's always wise to approach the medical system as a competent consumer, capable of making your own decisions. As a woman with a disability, the decision to have a child will be a major one, requiring that you examine many factors, such as finances, child care, timing, and parenting duties. Most likely, you will need to be creative in managing the physical aspects of being a parent, but the positive experience of motherhood will compensate for any difficulties.

20 Can I adopt a child now that I have a spinal cord injury?

Many families decide that adoption is the best way to have a child. Choosing the right agency is very important. All agencies should be accessible, and several visits will be necessary for you to be interviewed and to fill out the necessary paper work. Ask lots of questions relating to your disability, and determine what their attitude is. Has the agency placed children with parents who have disabilities? What is their attitude toward disabilities? Do they believe in consumer empowerment, or do they maintain a role of being experts? Finally, consider meeting with other parents who have used the agency to find out what their experience was and how the agency handled their disability issues.

Be prepared for a challenging, lengthy, and costly process. Agencies usually have orientation meetings that outline procedures and policies. You'll complete an application process that usually includes home study in which a caseworker visits and interviews you as a prospective parent. You will be asked how your disability will affect your parenting and what impact it might have on the child. You'll be evaluated on your ability to support and provide care for the child. If approved, you will then be placed on a list awaiting a child available for adoption. The waiting could take several months or years, depending on the particular agency and number of available children. After a child arrives, there are a series of evaluations and a court hearing. You will receive a new birth certificate with the child's new name and your name as the adoptive parent.

Adoption is an important option for people who want to have a child. The entire process can be expensive, frustrating, and bureaucratic, especially for people with disabilities. Often there will be prejudices toward people with disabilities, inaccessibility, and financial constraints. However, those people who are able to handle the difficulties will find it to be rewarding.

21 When should I consider genetic counseling?

Anyone with a physical disability that has a genetic or unknown cause should think about genetic counseling before having children. The counselor will be able to give information on prenatal testing and discuss the chances that your children will be born with a disability. The counselor will also be able to give information about certain treatments. Therapies may even be available to the unborn child to reduce disability.

The decision to have a child is yours, but the genetic counselor can give you helpful information. This is a very specialized area, and most doctors cannot provide you with the most accurate information. Ask for a referral to a special-ist, and make sure that the specialist has experience with people who have similar disabilities.

22 What would it be like to be pregnant with a spinal cord injury?

Women with spinal cord injuries have "normal" pregnancies, although they must be careful about potential complications and difficulties. For example, they must be cautious about urinary tract infections and developing anemia, which in-creases the risk of pressure sores. In addition, skin break-downs may become a greater problem as weight increases throughout the pregnancy. As this occurs, routines regarding weight shifting and pressure relief must change as well. Hyperreflexia is also a potential problem as the woman gets closer to her due date. Early delivery, or the inability to feel contractions signaling the onset of labor, can be managed by conservative treatment, such as weekly checkups.

For women who remain sexually active during their pregnancy, hyperreflexia can be reduced by limiting sex to once or twice a week. The male partner should also be en-couraged to decrease the force of his thrust and to use alter-natives to the missionary position to reduce the risk of pre-mature labor. In the third trimester, it is a good idea to reduce the frequency of sexual activity even further, and by the seventh month to discontinue sex altogether. After the birth, sexual activity for women with spinal cord injury can generally be resumed after 3–4 weeks, depending on the pain experienced by the woman. If the woman has had an episiotomy, it is recommended that she wait at least 4–5 weeks before resuming sexual activity.

23   Can I get pregnant from anal sex?

Absolutely not. With anal intercourse, the sperm is deposited in the rectum, not in the vagina or internal sexual organs. As a result, there is no chance of getting pregnant. For couples who enjoy anal intercourse, many women prefer to empty their bowel with an enema prior to sexual activity. In addition, using a lubricant can make it easier to insert the penis and reduce possible pain. To prevent the spread of bacteria, it is important to wash the penis after anal sex before engaging in oral sex or vaginal intercourse. It is generally recommended to use a condom for anal intercourse since the AIDS virus can easily be transmitted this way.

24   How do I know if I am in labor if I can't feel my body?

Women with injuries above T9 will generally not be aware of labor pains resulting from uterine contractions. But they may feel the onset as a result of other symptoms, such as bleeding and breaking of water. Women with injuries at or above T6 may get hyperreflexic during labor and need to be under close medical supervision to ensure safe blood-pressure levels. Because of the possibility of early labor, it is a good idea to have weekly checkups after Week 32 of your pregnancy. In addition, it is advisable to enter the hospital for monitoring and bed rest as soon as dilation begins. A close relationship with your obstetrician is your best insurance for a healthy and safe pregnancy.

25 Can I still breast-feed my baby after a spinal cord injury?

Some help with positioning may be necessary after your injury, but breast-feeding is still possible. Women with high-level spinal cord injuries may experience the most problems because of balance difficulties and limited arm and hand control. If your injury is above T6, milk production may shut down early and can stop approximately 6 weeks following delivery. In these women, nipple stimulation is necessary for continued milk production. In women who have decreased sensation in the nipple and breast area, milk production can be difficult because this mechanism is affected by the injury.

26 Can I be a good mother?

There is absolutely no reason you cannot be a great mother, regardless of your injury. Women with spinal cord injury report difficulties with motherhood as well as many successful solutions to problems they encounter. Many of the difficulties involve picking up the child and performing functions such as feeding, changing diapers, and bathing. During the early years, assistance will probably be more necessary than it will be later. Holding the child during breast-feeding may also be difficult, but it can be solved by proper positioning and assistance from family, partners, or personal care attendants. If you need advice or someone to talk with, your local independent living center may be able to link you up with mothers who have a disability. Also, take a good look at your home environment and consider changing it to make it as easy as possible for you to take care of your baby.

On an emotional level, it may be difficult for you to accept help with a function as personal and important as mothering your child. Feelings of guilt and sadness are also common in the early months following the birth of your child. Motherhood may remind you of many of the losses that you have endured since injury. For many women, the joy of motherhood can be a bittersweet experience at first, because of frustrations and guilt associated with raising a child with assistance from another person. Eventually, however, these feelings should pass, and the rewards of parenthood will overshadow them. Your maternal skills and your ability to nurture were not injured. You have as much potential to be a good mother as any other woman.

27 How can I be a father in a wheelchair?

A wheelchair does not subtract from your ability to be a good father. It may affect your ability to do physical activities with your children, but these activities are not the most critical part of being a father. You can still spend quality time with your children and share in almost every aspect of their childhood. Most important, you can still offer them the love and understanding that all children need. These are the critical components of being a father. The rest we've learned from TV and the movies. You might want to talk with someone else who uses a wheelchair and has children. Ask questions about the day-to-day activities. How do they ensure the safety of their children, change diapers, and play with the kids?

If you already have children, keep in mind that this will be a difficult time for them. They may feel like they have been forgotten in the turmoil of your injury and rehabilitation. Be careful not to take out your anger and emotions on them. Spend extra time with them, talk about your injury, let them ask questions, let them sit on your lap or bed, and let them try the wheelchair and be a part of everything going on. Most important, keep telling them how much you love them and offer them the reassurance that they need during this period of change.

28 Can my kids adjust to me being in a wheelchair?

Like yourself, your children may have a rocky adjustment initially. Your partner may need to take a more active role in parenting for a short time, while you make some of the early adjustments that are necessary in returning to your home and community. Your availability to your children will play a major role in determining how well they adjust. They may test your authority initially to see whether you can maintain the discipline that you did prior to your injury. They also need to know that you can be just as nurturing as before. This may be a difficult time for your children, and they may be more needy and dependent than ever. Issues like physical contact with you and fears of being left alone may remain for some time. With patience, however, they should be able to return to normal. Luckily, children are less rigid than grownups and will make necessary adjustments easier and quicker than adults.

5

Sexually Transmitted Diseases and Future Research

1. Can I still get AIDS and other sexually transmitted diseases?

2. How can I reduce the risk of contracting a sexually transmitted disease?

3. What is AIDS?

4. Sometimes I want a relationship so much I don't worry about AIDS. Is that so unusual?

5. Why do alcohol and drug use increase the chances of being infected with a sexually transmitted disease?

6. What are high-risk sexual activities?

7. How do I use a condom to make sure I don't get infected with AIDS?

8. Can I get AIDS from oral sex?

9. Can I get AIDS from making love to my lesbian partner?

10. Isn't AIDS primarily a problem for gay men?

11. Is research being done on the sexuality of women with spinal cord injury?

12. Is there any new research on men and sexuality?

1 Can I still get AIDS and other sexually transmitted diseases?

A spinal cord injury does nothing to protect you from getting sexually transmitted diseases (STDs). For instance, if you have sex or share needles or blood products with an infected person, you are at a high risk to acquire HIV and develop AIDS. Protect yourself as much as possible by learning about AIDS and using safer sex practices.

2 How can I reduce the risk of contracting a sexually transmitted disease?

Sexually transmitted diseases (e.g., AIDS, herpes, gonorrhea, syphilis, warts, disease caused by insects such as lice) are getting more common each day. Current estimates are that at least 50% of the population will have an STD at some time in their lives. While the best method of prevention is to avoid sexual contact with an infected person, sometimes there are no visible symptoms to warn a potential partner. Prevention can be enhanced by limiting the number of sexual partners you have and by using condoms every time. Also, make sure you know your partner well before engaging in sexual activity. It is also a good idea to be concerned about the cleanliness of your own genital area and to wash before and after sexual contact. Washing the penis and genital area is even more important if you use a wheelchair, since moisture easily collects and causes infection. Always look for open sores on yourself and your partner.

Bacterial diseases (e.g., syphilis, gonorrhea) and trichomoniasis (caused by a parasite passed through intercourse) can be cured. Viral STDs (e.g., AIDS, herpes, genital warts) cannot. Drugs can control herpes and genital warts, but abstaining from sexual contact is generally necessary when the virus is active. Herpes is considered to be as common among

women as men, and wearing a condom during an active out-
break is not an effective means of preventing the spread of
the virus. To minimize the risk of AIDS, where symptoms
are not visible for many years, a person must engage in sexual practices where there is no exchange of bodily fluids,
such as blood or semen.

3 What is AIDS?

AIDS stands for acquired immunodeficiency syndrome and
is caused by the human immunodeficiency virus (HIV). This
virus attacks the immune system so that it is no longer able
to fight off infections and diseases. It may take many years
for AIDS to affect the immune system after a person acquires
HIV. Symptoms may begin to appear up to 15 years after
infection. You cannot tell if a person has the virus without
medical testing. Today, it is expected that all people with
AIDS will eventually die because no treatments currently exist that can cure the disease.

4 Sometimes I want a relationship so much I don't worry about AIDS. Is that so unusual?

Many people want a relationship very badly and feel that
they will do almost anything to be close to another person.
Unfortunately, this attitude can be dangerous and lead to unhealthy and sometimes harmful situations. For example,
women who are abused may feel that they have no choice
but to remain in an unhealthy relationship. Men or women
may have an apathetic or indifferent attitude toward their
partner's health. This demonstrates little regard for your

own well-being and is a sign of depression and low feelings of self-worth. Typically, a relationship based on low self-esteem will not last, and individuals get hurt when one partner feels this desperate. If you feel this way, it's time to talk to someone.

5 Why do alcohol and drug use increase the chances of being infected with a sexually transmitted disease?

Alcohol and other drugs, although not dangerous in themselves (except for sharing a needle, a common way of contracting HIV), affect people's judgment. If you have been drinking, for example, you may not notice a sore on your partner's genitals, or you may not place a condom on correctly. Alcohol and other drugs could also affect your ability to ask questions regarding your partner's background. All of these could put you in danger of getting a sexually transmitted disease. Excessive use of alcohol and other drugs also can result in poor nutrition and health, which could weaken your resistance and your immune system.

6 What are high-risk sexual activities?

High-risk sexual activities greatly increase your chances of contracting the HIV virus. They include having vaginal or anal intercourse without a condom, sharing sex toys or needles, having oral contact with the rectum, or inserting large objects, such as your hand, into the rectum and tearing the lining of the anus. If you choose to have sex, it is important to find safe ways of doing so. While not 100% safe, condoms will greatly reduce the risk of getting AIDS if used properly.

Other activities, such as mutual masturbation, are relatively safe, as they do not involve the exchange of bodily fluids.

7 How do I use a condom to make sure I don't get infected with AIDS?

There is no 100% safe way to protect yourself other than abstaining from sexual activity with a partner. However, the correct use of a condom will greatly reduce the risk of HIV infection. Make sure that you or your partner put it on correctly for maximum protection. Sometimes it takes some practice getting on a condom and unrolling it down the penis. This is especially true if your partner is putting on the condom and is not very familiar with it. The condom must be on during the entire act of intercourse, since pre-ejaculatory fluid can also contain the virus. Always use a latex condom and not one that is porous or made of natural membranes. Use only a water-based lubricant, because a greasy lubricant damages the condom. If possible, use a foam or jelly that contains nonoxynol-9, a chemical that is believed to offer some protection against the AIDS virus. If the condom does break, you should wash the genital area and use a new one. Never use a condom more than once. Finally, when removing the condom, hold it by the rim and be careful not to spill the semen.

8 Can I get AIDS from oral sex?

Yes, you can. Any sexual contact that leads to an exchange of bodily fluids can transfer the AIDS virus. A woman whose male partner ejaculates in her mouth is at risk. Even before ejaculation, there is some fluid that can transmit the virus. A man giving oral stimulation to a female partner is at risk if she has the virus. A female partner of an HIV-positive woman is also at risk if she performs oral sex, although the rates of transmission this way are said to be lower. It is essential to use a condom or a dental dam to reduce the risk of disease transmission during oral sex.

9 Can I get AIDS from making love to my lesbian partner?

Yes, it is possible to get AIDS from another woman if you are a lesbian. If bodily fluids are exchanged, you are at risk. An infected partner's blood or vaginal lubrication can transmit the virus. However, there are many ways female partners can stimulate one another without risk: mutual masturbation, kissing, and stimulation with a vibrator, to name a few.

10 Isn't AIDS primarily a problem for gay men?

Certainly, the high-risk groups for HIV and AIDS are gay men and drug abusers who share needles. However, everyone who is sexually active risks contracting the AIDS virus. The exchange of any bodily fluid among any partners can be dangerous. This is why safe sex techniques have been stressed so much, especially if you do not know your partner well. These techniques include closed mouth kissing, mutual masturbation, manual stimulation (if there are no cuts on your hands), hugging, and using sex toys such as vibrators.

One final note: Although AIDS is a disease that we should all be aware of and extremely careful about, there has been much hysteria and discrimination against people with the disease. It is important to remember that you cannot contract HIV from toilet seats, coughing, shaking hands, and other activities of this nature. If you are careful, know your partners, and engage in safe sexual practices, there should be little worry about becoming infected.

11 Is research being done on the sexuality of women with spinal cord injury?

A number of important areas are being researched that affect women with a spinal cord injury. You may have heard of a controversial study describing a type of intense orgasm accompanied by a gush of fluids, the so-called "G-spot orgasm." The same researchers also propose that women have two pathways from the spinal cord to the genital area. These two pathways work together to result in a sexual response for the woman. When a woman has a spinal cord injury, one or both of these pathways may still be working, accounting for the fact that the majority of women with spinal cord injury can still respond sexually, have children, and menstruate.

Other research is exploring issues regarding the muscles around the vagina. If because of a spinal cord injury the woman's vagina tends to be loose, she may be able (depending on the level and completeness of the injury) to strengthen the muscles around the opening by doing Kegel exercises regularly. (Kegel exercises are performed by squeezing the muscles that control the flow of urine.) Medicines are also being researched that help keep the muscles strong and restore sensation in the genital area.

Orgasms require muscle contractions that are often affected by spinal cord injuries. Several types of oral and topical medicines and muscle-stimulating devices are being developed to treat weak contractions and to strengthen the woman's orgasm. Research is also seeking to understand exactly how women's sexual systems work and what effect spinal cord injury has on them. This includes questions about gynecological problems, pregnancy complications, the effect of menstrual cycles on spasticity, bladder and bowel functioning, and the effects of spinal cord injury on hormones.

Research on a woman's sexuality has been scant. In the late 1990s, however, this area has been designated as a priority by federal agencies such as the National Institute on Disability and Rehabilitation Research. As a result, women can anticipate major advances being made and more knowledge being provided to women with disabilities. Researchers are also frequently looking for women who are interested in taking part and serving as subjects in scientific studies related to sexual functioning. Check newsletters, independent living centers, and major academic rehabilitation centers to find out what might be available.

12 Is there any new research on men and sexuality?

This area has been the focus of much research and will continue to be for many years. In the field of spinal cord injury, most research is being conducted on issues of erections and fertility. Much of it is being done by urology departments at large university hospitals around the country. In the years ahead, oral pills or plasters placed on the penis will probably be used to enhance erection quality for many men. They will eliminate the injections, vacuums, and implants that are now available. Many of the drugs that are now experimental will become FDA approved and be available to a wider group of men with disabilities.

In the field of fertility, new methods of obtaining sperm are being developed that will make pregnancies more common after a spinal cord injury. For female partners, there are also new methods of in vitro fertilization being developed that will rely less on sperm quantity and motility—two major problems in spinal cord injury. In addition, researchers are investigating the effects of spinal cord injuries on sperm production and sperm quality, so that new treatments can be developed.

Appendix A

Glossary

Abstinence
Choosing not to engage in genital sexual activity.

AIDS
Acquired immunodeficiency syndrome, a fatal illness caused by the human immunodeficiency virus (HIV), which is transmitted by the exchange of bodily fluids.

Anus
The external opening of the body through which defecation (bowel movement) occurs and which can be an erogenous zone. Anal stimulation should be accompanied by good hygiene to prevent infection.

Anxiety
A physical and psychological state of tension and apprehension that may prevent a person from thinking clearly or taking action to solve problems. Anxiety may interfere with sexual functioning.

Autonomic hyperreflexia
A condition in which a full bladder or rectum causes high blood pressure, restlessness, chills, sweating, headache, fever, and slow heart beat. It requires emergency medical treatment.

Birth control pill	An oral contraceptive method that uses synthetic hormones to prevent the woman's egg from being released and thereby prevents pregnancy. It is effective and widely used but may have side effects. It is prescribed by a physician.
Bladder accident	A leakage of urine from the bladder.
Bladder infection	An inflammation of the urinary bladder causing pain, blood in urine, and frequent urgent urination. It is usually treated with antibiotics, drinking more liquids, and rest.
Bowel	Intestine; the part of the digestive system from the stomach to the anus where solid waste is formed before it is released through the rectum.
Breast	A complex organ of fatty and connective tissue that has three functions in women: sexual stimulation, self-concept/body image, and production of milk to feed an infant.
Caverject (alprostadil for injection)	A self-injection system with pre-filled syringes manufactured by Upjohn, available in 10 and 20 mg strengths and used to produce an erection. Caverject is available by prescription only, and its cost may be covered by some insurances.
Cervical region	The upper section of the spinal cord, which controls function in the neck and shoulders.
Cervix	That portion of the uterus that protrudes into the vagina.

Clitoris The area of a woman's sex organs that lies at the junction of the inner labia and is specialized to produce pleasure from direct or indirect stimulation.

Counseling A type of psychotherapy that emphasizes support or re-education.

Depression A condition marked by sadness, confusion, or difficulty thinking and lowered energy, which may include sleep disturbance, appetite changes, crying, and hopelessness.

Diabetes A disease affecting the body's sugar use caused by an inability to produce enough insulin or to use insulin properly. Difficulties in sexual functioning may result if circulation or nervous system complications develop.

Diaphragm A contraceptive method in which a rubber cup is inserted into the vagina to cover the cervix. Pregnancy is prevented because the sperm cannot reach the egg. It is used with contraceptive foam or gel, is effective, and has few side effects. It is fitted and prescribed by a physician.

Dildo A sex toy in the shape of a long cylinder, resembling a penis, used to produce sexual stimulation.

Dysfunction A term used that refers to things not working the way they are supposed to. "Sexual dysfunction" means problems with sex, including the inability to have orgasm, premature ejaculation, painful intercourse, the inability to get or maintain an erection, and the lack of sexual desire.

Ejaculation   The part of the sexual response in which semen is rhythmically expelled from the penis. It can occur with or without an erection and may be accompanied by orgasm.

Electroejaculation   A method of obtaining semen to be used in artificial insemination by using a powerful vibrator to cause ejaculation.

Endocrinologist   A physician who specializes in the diagnosis and treatment of hormonal disorders and who provides nonsurgical treatment of erection problems.

Estrogen   A sex hormone that regulates female development and menstrual cycles. It is produced by the ovaries and other organs.

Fallopian tubes   The part of the uterus that curves out toward the ovaries and directs the egg from the ovaries to the uterus.

Gay   A term used for both homosexual men and lesbian women, though more commonly only for men whose sexual orientation is toward men.

Genitals   The male or female sex organs. In men, the penis and scrotum are the external genitals. In women, the external sex organ is called the vulva, consisting of the inner and outer labia, the clitoris, the pubic mound, and the area of the vaginal and urinary openings. The genitals in men and women also consist of their sexual internal and reproductive organs.

Glans   The head of the penis.

Gynecologist   A physician who specializes in the health care of women.

Herpes II   A sexually transmitted disease caused by a virus and affecting the skins and moist linings of the mouth, nose, genitals, and rectum. It is passed by direct contact with the active sores.

Identity   The way a person defines him- or herself; the sense the individual has that allows him or her to relate to others and the environment. It includes body image, the concept one has of one's own body's structure, function, and appearance.

Implant   A surgical method in which silicone rods are placed in the spongy parts of the penis to stimulate erection, allowing men who are unable to get an erection to have intercourse.

Impotence   A medical term used to describe the inability to get or keep an erection, which may be due to physical or psychological causes or a combination of both.

Independent living center (ILC)   A rehabilitation program run by people with disabilities themselves, which provides consumers with personal assistance, ranging from home health care to help with activities of daily living. ILCs are based on the philosophy of the self-help movement, that people with disabilities have the ability and right to make their own decisions and to live their lives with the highest degree of independence possible.

Infertility   The inability to conceive children, which can affect both men and women.

Intercourse   A sexual act in which stimulation results from inserting the penis into the vagina and thrusting the pelvis.

IUD (intrauterine device)   A contraceptive device that is inserted into the uterus by a physician. It is made of metal or plastic and prevents pregnancy by irritating the lining of the uterus and thus preventing the egg from implanting.

Labia   The lips of the woman's sex organs. The labia majora and labia minora are the large outer lips and smaller inner lips of the woman's vulva, respectively (see *Genitals*). The outer lips may be covered with pubic hair, while the hairless inner lips may be especially sensitive to touch.

Lesbian   A woman whose sexual orientation is toward women.

Libido   Sexual desire; a complex and only partly understood aggregate of physical, emotional, and learned factors that result in sexual interest and behavior.

Lumbar region	The lower section of the spinal cord, which controls function in the lower trunk and legs.
Male superior position	A position for heterosexual intercourse in which the woman is on her back with the man on top of her, facing her; also called the missionary position.
Masturbation	Sexual self-stimulation.
Menopause	The cessation of menstruation. As a woman ages, hormone production and egg release decrease, until the monthly periods stop and pregnancy is no longer possible.
Menstruation	The monthly period during which the uterine lining and blood are shed; starts at puberty and ends at menopause.
Multiple sclerosis	A disease of the nervous system that affects the protective layer around nerve cells and diminishes the ability of messages to pass between the body and the brain. It often affects young adults ages 20–40, resulting in weakness of the limbs or other muscles, numbness, or visual problems. There is currently no cure, but experimental treatments are being found that help slow down the progression of the disease.
Nipples	The center part of the breast that hardens and enlarges during sexual stimulation in women and some men.
Oral sex	A sexual act in which stimulation results from licking, kissing, nibbling, or

sucking the partner's genitals. Cunnilingus refers to oral sex on the vagina; fellatio is oral sex on the penis.

Orgasm   The climax of sexual excitement, which physically consists of a release of neuromuscular tension. Subjectively, the experience of orgasm varies from one person to another, but is generally described as a pleasurable feeling of release in the genital area or throughout the body.

Ovaries   The parts of the woman's internal sex organs that lie on each side of the uterus. They produce eggs and the female hormones estrogen and progesterone.

Ovulation   The monthly release of an egg from the woman's ovaries.

Papaverine   A smooth muscle relaxant used to produce erections by means of injection therapy.

Peer counselor   A person who provides advice or guidance to a patient who has the same type of illness or injury that the counselor has successfully adjusted to.

Penis   The male sexual organ.

Physiatrist   A physician who specializes in physical medicine and rehabilitation.

**Premature
  ejaculation**   Sexual dysfunction in which the man has persistent inability to regulate his arousal toward ejaculation. He may be unaware of when he is about to ejaculate and unable to delay ejaculation

long enough for his pleasure or his partner's pleasure to build up.

Prostate gland   The gland that produces the majority of the fluid in the semen. The fluid nourishes the sperm and helps its motility. The prostrate surrounds the urethra, the tube that carries urine out of the body.

Psychiatrist   A physician (M.D.) who specializes in the prevention, diagnosis, and treatment of mental and emotional disorders. A psychiatrist may use psychotherapy and/or medications to accomplish the goals of treatment.

Psychologist   A person holding a doctoral degree (Ph.D., Psy.D., or Ed.D.) in psychology, who uses that training to diagnose and treat mental and emotional problems and behavior disorders. Psychologists are frequently trained to research human behavior and provide psychotherapy.

Psychotherapy   Treatment for mental illness, behavior disorders, or other problems of an emotional nature by establishing a professional relationship with a client for the purpose of modifying or removing symptoms or changing problematic patterns of behavior and promoting positive growth and development.

Puberty   The period during early adolescence during which boys and girls mature sexually.

Rehabilitation   The process by which people with physical disabilities acquire the skills

	necessary to become functionally independent and enjoy a greater quality of life.
Retrograde ejaculation	Ejaculation of the semen back into the bladder. If the bladder sphincter no longer works, semen does not come out of the penis. This condition doesn't reduce sexual pleasure or cause harm, but it does prevent fertility. Some men with paraplegia, those on some blood pressure medicines, and those who have had bladder or prostate surgery or radiation of the pelvis are among those likely to have retrograde ejaculation.
Sacral region	The lowest section of the spinal cord, which controls function in the bladder, bowel, and genital organs.
Scrotum	The sac that holds the testicles.
Semen	The liquid that is expelled from the penis during ejaculation. This liquid contains sperm and fluids produced by the prostate gland and seminal vesicles (two small pouches at the sides of the prostrate).
Seminal fluid	The sugary fluid produced by the seminal vesicles that makes up one component of semen.
Sensation	A feeling or awareness of bodily state that occurs when a nerve is stimulated and sends a signal to the brain.
Sex drive	Sexual desire, libido.

Social worker   An individual trained in social case work and treatment of children and adults whose personal and social problems are due to mental health issues or behavior problems. Social workers may assist patients via psychotherapy and/or practical help with housing, finances, insurance coverage, etc. Most social workers have a bachelor's or master's degree.

Spasticity   Uncontrolled muscle tightening and loss of muscular control.

Sperm   The tiny cells of male reproduction that, when ejaculated and united with the woman's egg, cause the egg to be fertilized, thus beginning pregnancy.

Spinal cord   A major part of the nervous system consisting of a long, nearly round cord reaching from the base of the skull to the lower back and surrounded by the vertebrae (bones). The spinal cord carries sense and movement signals to and from the brain and controls many reflexes.

Testicles   The part of the man's sexual organs that produce sperm and hormones (androgens, chiefly testosterone, and estrogen). They are the two round organs contained in the scrotum, or sac, under the penis.

Testosterone   The sex hormone that regulates male development, fertility, and desire. It is produced by the testicles and adrenal gland.

Thoracic region   The middle section of the spinal cord, which controls functions in the chest.

Transvestism   Cross-dressing. Transvestites are usually heterosexual men who find it pleasurable or comfortable to wear women's clothing.

Traumatic head injury   An injury caused by an accident (e.g., a fall, hitting a car windshield) or an assault (e.g., a bullet wound) that is serious enough to damage the brain.

Urethra   The canal that carries urine from the bladder to the outside of the body. In men, it also serves as the passageway for semen during ejaculation.

Urologist   A physician who specializes in the diagnosis and treatment of urinary tract disorders in men and women and of the male genital tract.

Uterus   The female organ that holds the developing fetus (baby) in a pregnant woman. It is a thick-walled and elastic organ whose lining provides nourishment for the fertilized egg; if the woman is not pregnant, this lining, which develops monthly, is shed during menstruation.

Vacuum device   A cylinder placed over the penis that creates a vacuum so that blood flows into the penis, producing a type of erection.

Vagina   The female sexual organ whose opening is at the vulva and that extends approximately 3–5 inches to the neck of the uterus (cervix). It becomes lubricated during sexual stimulation and is able to expand to permit insertion of the penis, fingers, or a dildo. It also expands during the birthing process for the baby to pass through.

Vaginismus   Sexual dysfunction in which the muscles surrounding the vaginal opening contract, preventing intercourse or causing intercourse to be painful.

Vas deferens   The narrow tubes that carry the sperm from the scrotum to be mixed with fluid in the prostate gland and the seminal vesicles (see *Semen*).

Vascular   Having to do with blood vessels.

Venereal disease   A sexually transmitted disease.

Venereal warts   Lesions on the external genitals, cervix, or anus caused by a virus passed through sexual contact with an infected partner. Some types may predispose women to cervical cancer.

Vulva   The female genitals, including clitoris, labia, and vagina.

Appendix B

Resources

American Association of Sex Educators, Counselors, and Therapists
435 North Michigan Avenue, Suite 1717
Chicago, IL 60611
(312) 644-0828 (Voice)

American Board of Sexology
1929 18th Street NW, Suite 1166
Washington, DC 20009
(202) 462-2122 (Voice & Fax)

Center for Sexual Function
Lahey Clinic North
One Essex Center Drive
Peabody, MA 01960
(508) 538-4655 (Voice)

Covenant Rehabilitation Center
Walter Verduyn, M.D.
2055 Kimball Avenue, Suite 120
Waterloo, IA 50702
(319) 234-0109 (Voice)

Handicap Introductions/ H.I. (National Computer Matching)
35 Wisconsin Circle, Suite 205
Chevy Chase, MD 20815
(301) 656-8723 (Voice)

Interdisciplinary Special Interest Group on Sexuality and Disability
American Congress of Rehabilitation Medicine
5700 Old Orchard Road
Skokie, IL 60077-1057
(708) 966-0095 (Voice)

National Council on Independent Living/ Access Living
310 South Peoria Street, Suite 201
Chicago, IL 60607
(312) 226-5900 (Voice)

National Rehabilitaiton Information Center and Able Data
8455 Colesville Road, Suite 935
Silver Spring, MD 20910
(301) 588-5900 (Voice)

National Spinal Cord Injury Association
245 Concord Avenue, Suite 29
Cambridge, MA 02138
(617) 441-8500 (Voice)

National Spinal Cord Injury Hotline
2201 Argonne Drive
Baltimore, MD 21218
(800) 526-3456 (Voice)

Paralyzed Veterans of America
801 18th Street NW
Washington, DC 20006
(202) USA-1300 (Voice)

Planned Parenthood National Headquarters
810 7th Avenue
New York, NY 10019
(800) 829-7732
(212) 541-7800 (Voice)

Sex Information and Education Counsel of the United States (SIECUS)
130 West 42nd Street, Suite 350
New York, NY 10036
(212) 819-9770 (Voice)

Sexuality and Disability Training Center
Boston University Medical Center
720 Harrison Avenue, Suite 906
Boston, MA 02118
(617) 638-7358 (Voice)

Sexuality and Disability Training Center
University of Michigan Medical Center
1500 East Medical Center Drive
Ann Arbor, MI 48109
(313) 936-7067 (Voice)

Appendix C

Independent Living Centers in the United States and Canada

UNITED STATES

Alabama

Birmingham Independent
    Living Center
206 13th Street, South
Birmingham, AL 35233
(205) 251-2223
TTY: 251-2223
FAX: 251-0605

Independent Living Center
5304 B Overlook Road
Mobile, AL 36618
(334) 460-0301
TTY: 460-2872
FAX: 460-0302

Alaska

Access Alaska, Inc.
3710 Woodland Drive, Suite
    900
Anchorage, AK 99517
(907) 248-4777
TTY: 248-8799
FAX: 248-0639

Hope Cottages, Inc.
540 West International
    Airport Road, Suite 100
Anchorage, AK 99518
(907) 561-5335
TTY: none
FAX: none

Within each state or province, addresses are listed alphabetically by city.

Access Alaska
3550 Airport Way, Suite 3
Fairbanks, AK 99709
(907) 479-7940
TTY: 479-7940
FAX: 479-4052

Independent Living
    Center—Homer
P.O. Box 2474
Homer, AK 99603
(907) 235-7911
TTY:235-7911
FAX: 235-6236

Southeast Alaska ILC (SAIL)
2490 Industrial Blvd.
Juneau, AK 99803
(907) 789-9665
TTY: 789-9665
FAX: 789-9747

Arizona

Arizona Bridge to
    Independent Living
1229 East Washington Street
Phoenix, AZ 85034
(602) 256-2245
TTY: 256-2245
FAX: 256-6407

New Horizons Independent
    Living Center, Inc.
8600 East Valley Road,
Suite B
Prescott Valley, AZ 86304
(520) 772-1266
TTY: None
FAX: 772-3808

DIRECT Center for
    Independence, Inc.
1023 North Tyndall Avenue
Tucson, AZ 85719
(520) 624-6452
TTY: 624:6452
FAX: 770-8522

Saguaro Maximizing
    Independent Living
1819 Maple Avenue
Yuma, AZ 85364
(520) 783-6069
TTY: 783-6069
FAX: 782-0061

Arkansas

Sources for Community IL
    Services, Inc.
212 East Poplar
Fayetteville, AR 72703
(501) 442-5600
TTY: 442:5600
FAX: 442-5192

Spa Area IL Services, Inc.
    (SAILS)
600 Main, Suite O
Hot Springs, AR 71913
(501) 624-7710
TTY: 624-7710
FAX: 624-7510

Mainstream Living
1818 South University
Little Rock, AR 72204
(501) 280-0012
TTY: 280-9262
FAX: 280-9267

Our Way, Inc.
10434 West 36th Street,
　Room 314
Little Rock, AR 72204
(501) 225-5030
TTY: 225-5030
FAX: none

Twin River Community
　Living Facility
201 Dodd Creek Road
Mountain Home, AR 72653
(501) 425-4515
TTY: none
FAX: none

Delta Resource Independent
　Living Center
400 South Main Street, Suite
　110
Pine Bluff, AR 71601
(501) 535-2222
TTY: 535-2222
FAX: 536-7713

California

Dayle McIntosh Center for
　the Disabled
150 West Cerritos, Bldg. 4
Anaheim, CA 92805
(714) 772-8285
TTY: 772-8366
FAX: 722-8292

Placer Independent Resource
　Services
11768 Atwood Road, Suite
　29
Auburn, CA 95603
(916) 885-6100
TTY: 885-0326
FAX: 885-3032

Independent Living Center
　of Kern County
1927 Eye Street
Bakersfield, CA 93301
(805) 325-1063
TTY: 325-3092
FAX: 325-6702

Center for Independence of
　the Disabled
875 O'Neill Avenue
Belmont, CA 94002
(415) 595-0783
TTY: 595-0743
FAX: 595-0261

Center for Independent
　Living
2539 Telegraph Avenue
Berkeley, CA 94704
(510) 841-4776
TTY: 848-3101
FAX: 841-6168

Central Coast Center for
　Independent Living
1395 41st Avenue, Suite B
Capitola, CA 95010
(408) 462-8720
TTY: 462-8720
FAX: 462-8727

IL Services of Northern
California
555 Rio Lindo Avenue,
Suite B
Chico, CA 95926
(916) 893-8527
TTY: 893-8527
FAX: 893:8574

Service Center for
Independent Living
P.O. Box 1296
Claremont, CA 91711
(909) 621-6722
TTY: (818) 967-4401
FAX: (818) 967-3132

San Gabriel Valley (Branch
Office)
963 West Badillo Street
Covina, CA 91722
(818) 967-0995
TTY: 967-4401
FAX: 967-3132

Southeast Center for IL
(SECIL)
12458 Rives Avenue, Room
202
Downey, CA 90242
(310) 862-6531
TTY: 869-0931
FAX: 923-5274

Humboldt Access Project,
Inc.
235 Fourth Street, Suite A
Eureka, CA 95501
(707) 445-8404
TTY: 445-8404
FAX: 445-9751

Center for Independent
Living in Fresno
3475 West Shaw Avenue,
Suite 101
Fresno, CA 93711
(209) 276-6777
TTY: 276-6779
FAX: 276-6778

F.R.E.E.D.
154 Hughes Road, Suite 1
Grass Valley, CA 95945
(916) 272-1732
TTY: 272-1733
FAX: 272-7793

Community Resources for
Independent Living
439 A Street
Hayward, CA 94541
(510) 881-5743
TTY: 881-0218
FAX: 881-1593

ILC of Southern California
(Branch Office)
356-B East Avenue, Suite 4
Lancaster, CA 93535
(805) 945-6602
TTY: 945-6604
FAX: 945-5690

Disabled Resources Center,
Inc.
2750 East Spring Street,
Suite 100
Long Beach, CA 90806
(310) 427-1000
TTY: 427-1386
FAX: 427-2027

Community Rehab
  Services—ILC
4716 Cesar Chavez,
Building B
Los Angeles, CA 90022
(213) 266-0453
TTY: 266-3016
FAX: 266-7992

Westside Center for
  Independent Living
12901 Venice Blvd.
Los Angeles, CA 90066
(310) 390-3611
TTY: 398-9204
FAX: 390-4906

IL Resource of Contra Costa
  County
3811 Alhambra Avenue
Martinez, CA 94553
(510) 229-9200
TTY: 229-9204
FAX: 229-1882

Modesto Center of
  Independent Living
1207 13th Street, Suite 2
Modesto, CA 95354
(209) 521-7260
TTY: 521-1425
FAX: 521-4763

Dayle McIntosh Center
  (Branch Office)
7223 Magnolia Avenue
Riverside, CA 92504
(909) 682-0230
TTY: 682-0232
FAX: 682-5224

Resources for Independent
  Living
1211 H Street, Suite B
Sacramento, CA 95814
(916) 446-3074
TTY: 446-3074
FAX: 446-3224

Central Coast CIL
234 Capitol Street, Suite A
Salinas, CA 93901
(408) 757-2968
TTY: 757-2968
FAX: 757-5549

Rolling Start, Inc.
570 West Fourth Street, Suite
  102
San Bernardino, CA 92401
(909) 884-2129
TTY: 884-7396
FAX: 386-7446

Access Center of San Diego,
  Inc.
1295 University Avenue,
  Suite 10
San Diego, CA 92103
(619) 293-3500
TTY: 293-7757
FAX: 293-3508

IL Resource Center San
  Francisco
70 Tenth Street
San Francisco, CA 94103
(415) 863-0581
TTY: 863-1367
FAX: 863-1290

Marin Center for
  Independent Living
710 Fourth Street
San Rafael, CA 94901
(415) 459-6245
TTY: 459-6245
FAX: 459-7047

Independent Living
  Resource Center
423 West Victoria
Santa Barbara, CA 93101
(805) 963-0595
TTY: 963-0595
FAX: 963-1350

Adult Independent
  Development Center
1601 Civic Center Drive,
  Suite 100
Santa Clara, CA 95050
(408) 985-1243
TTY: 985-9243
FAX: 985-0671

Community Resources for
  Independence
2999 Cleveland Avenue,
  Suite D
Santa Rosa, CA 95403
(707) 528-2745
TTY: 528-2151
FAX: 528-9477

The Mother Lode ILC
83 South Stewart, Suite 305
Sonora, CA 95370
(209) 532-0963
TTY: none
FAX: 532-0963

San Joaquin ILC
4505 Precissi Lane, Suite A
Stockton, CA 95207
(209) 477-7734
TTY: 477-7734
FAX: 477-7730

ILC of Southern California/
  Service Office
14354 Haynes
Van Nuys, CA 91401
(818) 988-9525
TTY: 988-3533
FAX: 785-0330

Independent Living Center
  of Southern California
14402 Haynes Street, Suite
  103
Van Nuys, CA 91401
(818) 785-6934
TTY: 785-7097
FAX: 785-0330

Colorado

San Luis Valley Center for
  Independent Living
P.O. Box 990
Alamosa, CO 81101
(719) 589-9660
TTY: none
FAX: none

Center for People with
  Disabilities
948 North Street, Suite 7
Boulder, CO 80304
(303) 442-8662
TTY: 442-8662
FAX: 442-0502

Colorado Springs
  Independence Center
21 East Las Animas
Colorado Springs, CO 80903
(719) 471-8181
TTY: 471-2076
FAX: 471-7829

Atlantis Community, Inc.
P.O. Box 9598
Denver, CO 80209
(303) 733-9324
TTY: 733-0047
FAX: 733-6211

Denver Center for
  Independent Living
777 Grant Street, Suite 100
Denver, CO 80203
(303) 837-1020
TTY: 837-1020
FAX: 837-0859

Southwest Center for
  Independence
3101 North Main Avenue
Durango, CO 81301
(303) 259-1672
TTY: none
FAX: 259-0947

Disabled Resource Services
424 Pine, Suite 101
Fort Collins, CO 80524
(970) 482-2700
TTY: 482-2723
FAX: 482-2723

Center for Independence
2829 North Avenue, Suite
  202
Grand Junction, CO 81501
(970) 241-0315
TTY: 241-8130
FAX: 245-3341

Greeley Center for
  Independence
1734 Eighth Avenue
Greeley, CO 80631
(970) 352-8484
TTY: none
FAX: 352-2074

Northern CO Center of
  Disability & Deafness
1024 Ninth Avenue, Suite E
Greeley, CO 80631
(970) 352-8682
TTY: 352-8682
FAX: 353-8058

Sangre de Cristo
  Independent Living
  Center
425 West Third Street
Pueblo, CO 81003
(719) 546-1271
TTY: 546-1867
FAX: 542-5456

Connecticut

Independence Northwest, Inc.
1183 New Haven Road, Suite 200
Naugatuck, CT 06770
(203) 729-3299
TTY: 729-1281
FAX: 729-2839

GNHDRA/Center Independence Access
One Long Wharf Drive, Suite 225
New Haven, CT 06511
(203) 562-3924
TTY: 624-5320
FAX: 624-6302

Chapel Haven, Inc.
1040 Whalley Avenue
New Haven, CT 06515
(203) 397-1714
TTY: none
FAX: 397-8004

Disabilities Network of Eastern Connecticut
107 Route Thirty Two
North Franklin, CT 06254
(860) 823-1898
TTY: 823-1898
FAX: 886-2316

Independence Unlimited, Inc.
2138 Silas Deane Highway, #2
Rocky Hill, CT 06067
(860) 257-3221
TTY: 257-3221
FAX: 257-3329

CIL of Southwestern Connecticut
80 Ferry Blvd.
Stratford, CT 06497
(203) 378-6977
TTY: 378-3248
FAX: 375-2748

New Horizons, Inc.
37 Bliss Memorial Road
Unionville, CT 06085
(203) 675-4711
TTY: none
FAX: 675-4369

District of Columbia

D.C. Center for Independent
  Living
1400 Florida Avenue
  Northeast, Suite 3
Washington, DC 20002
(202) 388-0033
TTY: 388-0033
FAX: 398-3018

Delaware

Easter Seal Independent
  Living Center
52 Read's Way
New Castle, DE 19720
(302) 324-4488
TTY: 324-4482
FAX: 324-4481

Independent Living, Inc.
1800 North Broom Street,
  Suite 210
Wilmington, DE 19802
(302) 429-6693
TTY: 429-8034
FAX: 429-8031

Florida

SCCIL
331 Ramp Road
Cocoa Beach, FL 32931
(407) 784-9008
TTY: 784-9008
FAX: 784-3702

SW Florida Coalition for IL,
  Inc.
3626 Evans Avenue
Fort Myers, FL 33901
(813) 277-1447
TTY: 277-3964
FAX: 277-1647

Broward Center for
  Independent Living, Inc.
2800 West Oakland Park,
  Suite 204
Fort Lauderdale, FL 33311
(305) 733-5592
TTY: 733-5592
FAX: 733-1554

Briarwood Center for
  Independent Living
1023 Southeast Fourth
  Avenue
Gainesville, FL 32601
(352) 378-7474
TTY: 376-1237
FAX: 378-5582

Opportunities Development,
    Inc., CIL
5243 Beach Blvd.
Jacksonville, FL 32207
(904) 399-8484
TTY: 399-8484
FAX: 396-0859

SFADA, Inc.
1335 NW 14th Street
Miami, FL 33125
(305) 325-0901
TTY: 325-0901
FAX: 547-7355

CIL of Northwest Florida,
    Inc.
513 East Fairfield Drive
Pensacola, FL 32503
(904) 435-9343
TTY: 435-9328
FAX: 435-1542

Suncoast Center for
    Independent Living
1945 Northgate Blvd.
Sarasota, FL 34234
(813) 351-9545
TTY: 351-9943
FAX: 351-9875

Caring and Sharing CIL, Inc.
1130 94th Avenue, North
St. Petersburg, FL 33702
(813) 577-0065
TTY: 576-5034
FAX: 577-2932

CIL of North Florida
572C Appleyard Drive
Tallahassee, FL 32304
(904) 575-9621
TTY: 576-5245
FAX: 575-5740

Self-Reliance, Inc., Center for
    Independent Living
12310 North Nebraska
    Avenue, Suite F
Tampa, FL 33612
(813) 975-6560
TTY: 975-6636
FAX: 975-6559

Coalition for Independent
    Living Options
2328 South Congress
    Avenue, Suite 1-F
West Palm Beach, FL 33406
(407) 966-4288
TTY: 641-6538
FAX: 641-6619

CIL in Central Florida, Inc.
720 North Denning Drive
Winter Park, FL 32789
(407) 623-1070
TTY: 623-1185
FAX: 628-5981

Georgia

Disability Action Center of
  Georgia
246 Sycamore Street, Suite
  100
Decatur, GA 30030
(404) 687-8890
TTY: 687-9175
FAX: 687-8298

LIFE, Inc.
17-19 East Travis Street
Savannah, GA 31406
(912) 920-2414
TTY: 920-2414
FAX: 920-0007

Hawaii

Center for Independent
  Living-East Hawaii
1190 Waianuenue Avenue
Hilo, HI 96720
(808) 935-3777
TTY: 935-3777
FAX: 961-6737

Hawaii Center for
  Independent Living
677 Ala Moana Blvd., Suite
  101
Honolulu, HI 96813
(808) 537-1941
TTY: 521-4400
FAX: 599-4851

Center for Independent
  Living-West Hawaii
P.O. Box 2197
Kealakekua, HI 96750
(808) 323-2221
TTY: 323-2262
FAX: 323-2383

Kauai CIL (Satellite Office)
P.O. Box 3529
Lihue, HI 96766
(808) 245-4034
TTY: 245-4164
FAX: none

Maui CIL (Satellite Office)
1464 Lower Main Street,
  Suite 105
Wailuku, HI 96793
(808) 242-4966
TTY: 242-4968
FAX: 244-6978

Idaho

Eastern Idaho Center for
  Independence
P.O. Box 86
Blackfoot, ID 83221
(208) 785-9648
TTY: none
FAX: 785-9648

Living Independence
  Network Corp.
708 West Franklin Street
Boise, ID 83702
(208) 336-3335
TTY: 336-3335
FAX: 384-5037

Disability Action Center-NW
124 East Third Street
Moscow, ID 83843
(208) 883-0523
TTY: 883-0523
FAX: 883-0524

Housing Southwest No. 2—
  Payette, Idaho
1108 West Finch Drive
Nampa, ID 83651
(208) 467-7461
TTY: none
FAX: none

Access for Idaho
P.O. Box 4185
Pocatello, ID 83201
(208) 232-2747
TTY: 232-2747
FAX: 232-2753

LINC (Branch Office)
1002 Shoshone Street, East
Twin Falls, ID 83301
(208) 733-1712
TTY: 733-1712
FAX: 733-7711

Illinois

Impact Center for
  Independent Living
2735 East Broadway
Alton, IL 62002
(618) 462-1411
TTY: 462-1411
FAX: 474-5309

LINC, Inc.
120 East A Street
Belleville, IL 62220
(618) 235-9988
TTY: 235-0451
FAX: 235-9244

Living Independence for
  Everyone CIL
1328 East Empire Street
Bloomington, IL 61701
(309) 663-5433
TTY: 663-5433
FAX: 663-7024

Center for Comprehensive
  Services
P.O. Box 2825
Carbondale, IL 62902
(618) 529-3060
TTY: none
FAX: none

Southern Illinois Center
for Independent
Living
P.O. Box 627
Carbondale, IL 62903
(618) 457-3318
TTY: 457-3318
FAX: 549-0132

Access Living of Metro
Chicago
310 South Peoria, Suite 201
Chicago, IL 60607
(312) 226-5900
TTY: 226-1687
FAX: 226-2030

Fox River Valley Center for
Independent Living
730 West Chicago Street
Elgin, IL 60123
(708) 695-5818
TTY: 695-5868
FAX: 695-5892

Will Grundy Center for
Independent Living
2415A West Jefferson Street
Joliet, IL 60435
(815) 729-0162
TTY: 729-2085
FAX: 729-3697

OPTIONS Center for
Independent Living
61 Meadowview Center
Kankakee, IL 60901
(815) 936-0100
TTY: 936-0132
FAX: 936-0117

Dupage Center for
Independent Living
400 East 22nd Street, Suite F
Lombard, IL 60148
(708) 916-9666
TTY: 916-9666
FAX: 916-9688

Opportunities for Access
3300 Broadway, Suite 5
Mt. Vernon, IL 62864
(618) 244-9212
TTY: 244-9575
FAX: 244-9310

Lake County Center for
Independent Living
706 East Hawley
Mundelein, IL 60060
(708) 949-4440
TTY: 949-4440
FAX: 949-4445

Progress Center for
Independent Living
320 Lake Street
Oak Park, IL 60302
(708) 524-0600
TTY: 524-0690
FAX: 524-1640

Central Illinois Center for
Independence
614 West Glen
Peoria, IL 61614
(309) 682-3500
TTY: 682-3500
FAX: 682-3989

Northwestern Illinois Center
    for IL
229 First Street, Suite 2
Rock Falls, IL 61071
(815) 625-7860
TTY: 625-7863
FAX: 625-7876

Illinois-Iowa Independent
    Living Center
P.O. Box 6156
Rock Island, IL 61204
(319) 324-1460
TTY: 324-1460
FAX: 324-1036

RAMP
1040 North Second Street,
    Lower Level
Rockford, IL 61107
(815) 968-7467
TTY: 968-2401
FAX: 968-7612

Springfield Center for
    Independent Living
426 West Jefferson
Springfield, IL 62702
(217) 523-2587
TTY: 523-6304
FAX: 523-0427

PACE, Inc.
1317 East Florida
Urbana, IL 61801
(217) 344-5433
TTY: 344-5024
FAX: 344-2414

Indiana

Damar Homes, Inc.
P.O. Box 41
Camby, IN 46113
(317) 856-5201
TTY: none
FAX: 856-2333

League for the Blind &
    Disabled, Inc.
5800 Fairfield, Suite 210
Fort Wayne, IN 46807
(219) 745-5491
TTY: 745-5491
FAX: 745-2202

Indianapolis Resource CIL
8383 Craig Street, Suite 130
Indianapolis, IN 46250
(317) 596-6440
TTY: 596-6440
FAX: 596-6446

Everybody Counts, Inc.
6701 Broadway
Merrillville, IN 46410
(219) 769-5055
TTY: 769-5008
FAX: 769-5325

Iowa

Central Iowa Center of
  Independent Living
1024 Walnut Street
Des Moines, IA 50309
(515) 243-1742
TTY: 243-2177
FAX: 243-5385

Evert Conner Rights &
  Resources CIL
20 East Market Street
Iowa City, IA 52245
(319) 338-3870
TTY: 338-3870
FAX: 338-8385

Illinois-Iowa Independent
  Living Center*
P.O. Box 6156
Rock Island, IL 61204
(319) 324-1460
TTY: 324-1460
FAX: 324-1036

Hope Haven
1800 19th Street
Rock Valley, IA 51247
(712) 476-2737
TTY: None
FAX: 476-2802

Kansas

Cowley County
  Developmental Services
P.O. Box 133
Arkansas City, KS 67005
(316) 442-3575
TTY: None
FAX: none

LINK, Inc.
202 Centennial Center
Hays, KS 67601
(913) 625-6942
TTY: 625-6942
FAX: 625-6137

Coalition For Independence
4631 Orville, #102
Kansas City, KS 66102
(913) 287-0999
TTY: 287-0999
FAX: 287-5726

Independence, Inc.
1910 Haskell
Lawrence, KS 66046
(913) 841-0333
TTY: 841-1046
FAX: 841-1094

Resource Center for
  Independent Living
210 North Ninth
Osage City, KS 66523
(913) 528-3105
TTY: 528-3106
FAX: 528-3665

Independent Connection
1710 West Schilling Road
Salina, KS 67401
(913) 827-9383
TTY: 827-9383
FAX: none

*Located in Illinois and also serving Iowa.

Independent Living
  Program (677/117A)
2200 Gage Blvd., VA
  Medical Center
Topeka, KS 66622
(913) 271-4350
TTY: none
FAX: none

Topeka IL Resource Center
501 Southwest Jackson, #100
Topeka, KS 66603
(913) 233-4572
TTY: 233-4572
FAX: 233-1561

Three Rivers IL Resource
  Center
408 Lincoln Avenue
Wamego, KS 66547
(913) 456-9915
TTY: 456-9915
FAX: 456-9923

ILC of Southcentral Kansas,
  Inc.
3330 West Douglas, Suite
  101
Wichita, KS 67203
(316) 942-6300
TTY: 942-6300
FAX: 942-2078

Kentucky

Contact, Inc.
103 Bridge Street
Frankfort, KY 40601
(502) 875-5777
TTY: none
FAX: none

Center for Accessible Living
981 South Third Street, Suite
  102
Louisville, KY 40203
(502) 589-6620
TTY: 589-3980
FAX: 589-3980

West End Awareness
3231 Larkwood, Suite 1
Louisville, KY 40212
(502) 776-4010
TTY: none
FAX: none

Center for Independent
  Living (Murray office)
104 North Fifth Street, Suite
  203
Murray, KY 42071
(502) 759-9227
TTY: 759-9227
FAX: 759-9227

Center for Accessible Living
1304U Chestnut Street
Murray, KY 42071
(502) 753-7676
TTY: 753-7729
FAX: 753-7729

Louisiana

New Horizons (Satellite
  Office)
1758 Elliott Street, Suite 2
Alexandria, LA 71301
(318) 484-3596
TTY: none
FAX: 484-3596

Resources for Independent
  Living (Satellite Office)
701 Main Street
Baton Rouge, LA 70802
(504) 379-3840
TTY: 379-3840
FAX: 379-3845

Southwest Louisiana
  Independence Center
3505 Fifth Avenue, Suite A2
Lake Charles, LA 70605
(318) 477-7194
TTY: 477-7196
FAX: 477-7198

Volunteers of America—
  Independent Living
3900 North Causeway Blvd.,
  Suite 750
Metairie, LA 70002
(504) 834-7015
TTY: none
FAX: none

New Horizons (Satellite
  Office)
2000A Tower Drive
Monroe, LA 71201
(318) 323-4374
TTY: none
FAX: 323-5445

Independent Living Center,
  Inc.
320 North Carrollton
  Avenue, Suite 2C
New Orleans, LA 70119
(504) 484-6400
TTY: 484-6400
FAX: none

Resources for Independent
  Living
1001 Howard Avenue, Suite
  1100
New Orleans, LA 70113
(504) 522-1955
TTY: 522-1956
FAX: 533-1954

New Horizons, Inc.
6502 St. Vincent
Shreveport, LA 71106
(318) 865-1000
TTY: 865-1088
FAX: 865-1092

Maine

Alpha One (Branch Office)
475 Western Avenue, Suite 13
Augusta, ME 04330
(207) 623-1115
TTY: 623-1115
FAX: 623-1369

Maine Independent Living
    Services
424 Western Avenue
Augusta, ME 04330
(207) 622-5434
TTY: 622-5434
FAX: 622-6947

Motivational Services, Inc./
    LINC Program
114 State Street
Augusta, ME 04330
(207) 626-3465
TTY: 626-3465
FAX: 626-3469

The Together Place
150 Union Street
Bangor, ME 04401
(207) 941-2907
TTY: none
FAX: none

Alpha One (Branch Office)
41 Acme Road, Suite 5
Brewer, ME 04412
(207) 989-6016
TTY: 989-6016
FAX: 989-7976

Shalom House, Inc.
90 High Street
Portland, ME 04101
(207) 874-1080
TTY: none
FAX: none

Alpha One (Branch Office)
373 Main Street, Suite 1
Presque Isle, ME 04769
(207) 764-6466
TTY: 764-6466
FAX: 764-5396

Alpha One
127 Main Street
South Portland, ME 04106
(207) 767-2189
TTY: 767-2189
FAX: 799-8346

Maryland

Maryland Center for
    Independent Living
6305-A Sherwood Road
Baltimore, MD 21239
(410) 377-5900
TTY: 377-4591
FAX: 377-4591

Independence Now, Inc.
818 Roeder Road, Suite 202
Silver Spring, MD 20910
(301) 587-4162
TTY: 587-4162
FAX: 587-4164

Massachusetts

Stavros Center for
 Independent Living, Inc.
691 South East Street
Amherst, MA 01002
(413) 256-0473
TTY: 256-0473
FAX: none

Boston Center for
 Independent Living
95 Berkeley Street, Suite 206
Boston, MA 02116
(617) 338-6665
TTY: 338-6662
FAX: 338-6661

Student IL Experience; MA
 Hospital
5 Randolph Street
Canton, MA 02021
(617) 828-2440
TTY: none
FAX: none

Southeast Center for
 Independent Living, Inc.
170 Pleasant Street, Third
 Floor East
Fall River, MA 02721
(508) 679-9210
TTY: 679-9210
FAX: 677-2377

Metro West Center for
 Independent Living
63 Fountain, Suite 504
Framingham, MA 01701
(508) 875-7853
TTY: 875-7853
FAX: 875-8359

ARC—Independent Living
 Program
101 Grove Street
Hyannis, MA 02601
(508) 771-6595
TTY: none
FAX: none

Cape Organization for
 Rights of the Disabled
114 Enterprise Road
Hyannis, MA 02601
(508) 775-8300
TTY: 775-8300
FAX: 775-7022

The Northeast Independent
 Living Program, Inc.
20 Ballard Road
Lawrence, MA 01843
(508) 687-4288
TTY: 687-4288
FAX: 689-4488

Renaissance Program
21 Branch Street
Lowell, MA 01851
(508) 454-7944
TTY: none
FAX: none

ILC of North Shore & Cape
 Ann
583 Chestnut Street
Lynn, MA 01904
(617) 593-7500
TTY: 593-7500
FAX: 595-1830

Ad LIB, Inc
442 North Street
Pittsfield, MA 01201
(413) 442-7047
TTY: 442-7194
FAX: 443-4338

Independence Association,
  Inc.
9 Taunton Green
Taunton, MA 02780
(508) 880-5325
TTY: 880-5325
FAX: 880-1163

Center for Living and
  Working, Inc.
484 Main Street, #345
Worcester, MA 01608
(508) 798-0350
TTY: 798-0350
FAX: 798-4015

Michigan

Ann Arbor Center for
  Independent Living
2568 Packard Georgetown
  Mall
Ann Arbor, MI 48104
(313) 971-0277
TTY: 971-0310
FAX: 971-0826

Great Lakes/Oakland
  Macomb Rehab. Corp.
4 East Alexandrine, Suite 104
Detroit, MI 48201
(313) 832-3371
TTY: 832-3372
FAX: 832-3850

Southeastern Michigan CIL
1200 Sixth Avenue, 15th
  Floor, South Tower
Detroit, MI 48226
(313) 256-1524
TTY: none
FAX: 256-1519

The Disability Network
877 East Fifth Avenue,
  Building D
Flint, MI 48503
(810) 239-7634
TTY: 239-7637
FAX: 239-7661

Grand Rapids Center for
  Independent Living
3600 Camelot Drive,
  Southeast
Grand Rapids, MI 49546
(616) 949-1100
TTY: 949-1100
FAX: 949-7865

Lakeshore Center for
  Independent Living
720 East Eighth, Suite 3
Holland, MI 49423
(616) 396-5326
TTY: 396-5326
FAX: 396-3220

Disability Resource Center
4026 South Westnedge
Kalamazoo, MI 49008
(616) 345-1516
TTY: 345-1516
FAX: 345-0229

Life Skills Services
1608 Lake Street
Kalamazoo, MI 49001
(616) 344-0202
TTY: none
FAX: 344-0285

Center of Handicapped
   Affairs
3815 West St. Joseph
   Highway, Suite D
Lansing, MI 48917
(517) 334-7832
TTY: 334-7828
FAX: 334-7849

Cristo Rey Hispanic Center
   for IL
1717 North High Street
Lansing, MI 48906
(517) 372-4700
TTY: 372-4700
FAX: none

Center for Independent
   Living of Mid-Michigan
1206 James Savage
Midland, MI 48640
(517) 835-4041
TTY: 835-4041
FAX: 835:8121

Blue Water Center for
   Independent Living
804 Huron Avenue
Port Huron, MI 48060
(810) 987-9337
TTY: 987-9337
FAX: 987-9548

Oakland/Macomb Center
   for Independent Living
3765 East 15 Mile Road
Sterling Heights, MI 48310
(810) 268-4160
TTY: 268-4520
FAX: 268-4720

Grand Traverse Area
   Community Living
935 Barlow
Traverse City, MI 49684
(616) 941-7150
TTY: none
FAX: 941-3421

Minnesota

Independence Crossroads,
   Inc.
8932 Old Cedar Avenue,
   South
Bloomington, MN 55425
(612) 854-8004
TTY: none
FAX: 854-7842

CIL of Northeastern
   Minnesota (Branch Office)
205 West Second Street,
   Suite 200
Duluth, MN 55802
(218) 722-8911
TTY: 722-8911
FAX: none

OPTIONS Resource Center
of Independent Living
318 Third Street, Northwest
East Grand Forks, MN 56721
(218) 773-6100
TTY: 773-6100
FAX: 773-7119

CIL of Northeastern
Minnesota, Inc.
Mesabi Mall
Hibbing, MN 55746
(218) 262-6675
TTY: 262-6675
FAX: 262-6677

Southern Minnesota IL
Enterprises & Services
709 South Front Street
Mankato, MN 56001
(507) 345-7139
TTY: 345-7139
FAX: 345-8429

Southwestern Center
for Independent
Living
109 South Fifth
Marshall, MN 56258
(507) 532-2221
TTY: 532-2221
FAX: 532-2222

Courage Center
3915 Golden Valley Road
Minneapolis, MN 55422
(612) 520-0235
TTY: 520-0410
FAX: 520-0577

Functional Independence
Training
2344 Nicollet Avenue, Suite
420
Minneapolis, MN 55404
(612) 871-4788
TTY: 871-4788
FAX: 871-5403

FREEDOM Resource Center
of IL
P.O. Box 917
Moorehead, MN 56561
(218) 236-0459
TTY: 236-0459
FAX: 236-0510

Southeastern Minnesota CIL,
Inc.
1306 Seventh Street,
Northwest
Rochester, MN 55901
(507) 285-1815
TTY: 285-0616
FAX: 288-8070

Central MN Care Center,
Inc., CIL
600 25th Avenue South,
Suite 110
St. Cloud, MN 56301
(612) 255-1882
TTY: 255-1882
FAX: none

Accessible Space, Inc.
2550 University Avenue
West, Suite 330N
St. Paul, MN 55114
(612) 645-7271
TTY: 800-466-7722
FAX: 645-0541

Metropolitan Center of
  Independent Living, Inc.
1600 University Avenue
  West, Suite 16
St. Paul, MN 55104
(612) 646-8342
TTY: 603-2001
FAX: 603-2006

Mississippi

Jackson Independent Living
  Center
300 Capers Avenue
Jackson, MS 39203
(601) 961-4140
TTY: 961-4140
FAX: 354-6678

Life, Inc.
754 North President Street,
  Suite 1
Jackson, MS 39202
(601) 969-4009
TTY: 969-4009
FAX: 969-1662

Gulf Coast Independent
  Living Center
P.O. Box 377
Long Beach, MS 39560
(601) 864-3786
TTY: 864-3786
FAX: none

Starkville Center of
  Independent Living
P.O. Drawer 6321
10 Montgomery Hall,
  MSU
Starkville, MS 39762
(601) 325-8511
TTY: 325-8511
FAX: none

Missouri

SEMO Alliance for
  Disability Independence,
  Inc.
121 South Broadview, Suite
  12
Cape Girardeau, MO 63703
(314) 651-6464
TTY: 651-6464
FAX: 651-6565

Services for Independent
  Living
1301 Vandiver Drive,
Suite Q
Columbia, MO 65202
(314) 874-1646
TTY: 874-4121
FAX: 874-3564

Access II Independent
  Living Center
102 North Main Street
Gallatin, MO 64640
(816) 663-2423
TTY: none
FAX: 663-2615

Rehabilitation Institute
3011 Baltimore
Kansas City, MO 64108
(816) 756-2250
TTY: 756-2250 ext. 221
FAX: 758-1884

The WHOLE PERSON, Inc.
3100 Main, Suite 206
Kansas City, MO 64111
(816) 561-0304
TTY: 531-7749
FAX: 753-8163

Rural Advocates for
  Independent Living
715 South Baltimore
Kirksville, MO 63501
(816) 627-7245
TTY: 627-0614
FAX: 627-0525

Southwest Center for
  Independent Living
1856 East Cinderella
Springfield, MO 65804
(417) 886-1188
TTY: 886-1188
FAX: 886-3619

Independence Center
4380 West Pine Blvd.
St. Louis, MO 63108
(314) 533-6511
TTY: none
FAX: 531-7372

Life Skills Foundation
10176 Corporate Square
  Drive, Suite 100
St. Louis, MO 63132
(314) 567-7705
TTY:567-7705 ext. 350
FAX: 567-6539

Paraquad
311 North Lindbergh Blvd.
St. Louis, MO 63141
(314) 567-1558
TTY: 567-5552
FAX: 567-1559

Disabled Citizens Alliance
  for Independence
P.O. Box 675
Viburnum, MO 65566
(314) 244-3315
TTY: 244-3315
FAX: 244-5609

Montana

Living Independently /
  Today & Tomorrow, Inc.
3116 First Avenue, North
Billings, MT 59101
(406) 259-5181
TTY: 259-1498
FAX: 259-5259

North Central IL Services,
  Inc.
104 Second Street, South,
  Suite 101
Great Falls, MT 59405
(406) 452-9834
TTY: 452-9834
FAX: 453-3940

Summit Ravalli County
  Office (Branch)
140 Cherry Street, Suite 5
Hamilton, MT 59840
(406) 363-5242
TTY: 363-5242
FAX: 363-5242

Montana Independent
  Living Project
38 South Last Chance Gulch
Helena, MT 59601
(406) 442-5755
TTY: 442-5756
FAX: 442-1612

Summit Flathead County
  Office (Branch)
275 Corporate Avenue, Suite
  901
Kalispell, MT 59901
(406) 257-0048
TTY: 257-0048
FAX: 257-0048

Summit Independent Living
  Center
1900 Brooks Street, Suite 120
Missoula, MT 59801
(406) 728-1630
TTY: 728-1630
FAX: 728-1632

Summit Lake County Office
  (Branch)
318 Main Street, Southwest
Ronan, MT 59864
(406) 676-0190
TTY: 676-0190
FAX: none

Nebraska

CIL of Central Nebraska,
  Inc.
1804 South Eddy
Grand Island, NE 68801
(308) 382-9255
TTY: 382-9255
FAX: 384-9231

League of Human Dignity,
  Inc.
1701 P Street
Lincoln, NE 68508
(402) 441-7871
TTY: 441-7871
FAX: 441-7650

League of Human Dignity
  ILC (Branch)
604 West Benjamin
Norfolk, NE 68701
(402) 371-4475
TTY: 371-4475
FAX: 371-4625

League of Human Dignity
  ILC (Branch)
5513 Center Street
Omaha, NE 68106
(402) 558-3411
TTY: 558-3411
FAX: 558-4609

Nevada

Nevada Association for
  Handicapped; IL Project
6200 West Oakey
Las Vegas, NV 89102
(702) 870-7050
TTY: 870-7050
FAX: 870-7649

Northern Nevada Center for
  Independent Living
999 Pyramid Way
Sparks, NV 89431
(702) 353-3599
TTY: 353-3599
FAX: 353-3588

New Hampshire

Granite State IL Foundation
P.O. Box 7268
Concord, NH 03301
(603) 228-9680
TTY: 228-9680
FAX: 225-3304

Granite State IL Foundation-
  North Country
P.O. Box 871
Franconia, NH 03580
(603) 823-5772
TTY: 823-5772
FAX: none

Granite State IL Foundation-
  Portsmouth
75 Congress Street
Portsmouth, NH 03801
(603) 430-3060
TTY: 430-3060
FAX: 430-3059

New Jersey

Success Through
  Independent Living
  Experience
1501 Park Avenue, Suite 1
Asbury Park, NJ 07712
(908) 774-0717
TTY: none
FAX: none

Camden City Independent
  Living Center
2101 Ferry Avenue, Suite 512
Camden, NJ 08104
(609) 962-0100
TTY: 962-0101
FAX: 962-0101

DIAL, Inc.
66 Mt. Prospect Avenue,
  Bldg. C
Clifton, NJ 07013
(201) 470-8090
TTY: 470-2521
FAX: 470-8171

Alliance for Disabled in
  Action
2050 Oak Tree Road
Edison, NJ 08820
(908) 321-1600
TTY: 321-1600
FAX: 321-1603

Total Living Center, Inc.
P.O. Box 342
Egg Harbor City, NJ 08215
(609) 965-3734
TTY: 965-5390
FAX: 965-1270

Heightened Independence &
  Progress (HIP)
131 Main Street, Suite 120
Hackensack, NJ 07601
(201) 996-9100
TTY: 996-9424
FAX: 996-9422

Heightened Independence &
  Progress (HIP)
2815 Kennedy Blvd., Suite 2G
Jersey City, NJ 07306
(201) 413-1200
TTY: 413-0521
FAX: 413-0520

Monmouth/Ocean
  Independent Living Center
279 Broadway, First Floor
Long Beach, NJ 07740
(908) 571-4884
TTY: 571-4878
FAX: 571-4003

Resources for Independent
   Living
115 Centerton Road, Suite 6,
   Masonville Square
Mt. Laurel, NJ 08054
(609) 273-7630
TTY: 273-3718
FAX: 273-3798

DIAL, Inc. (Northwest
   Branch)
#7 Boardwalk
Sparta, NJ 07861
(201) 729-7155
TTY: 729-3396
FAX: 729-5889

CIL for Mercer &
   Hunterdon County, Inc.
P.O. Box 8898
Trenton, NJ 08650
(609) 448-2998
TTY: 448-5821
FAX: 448-7293

CIL of South Jersey, Inc.
800 North Delsea Drive,
   Plaza 47, Suite 6
Westville, NJ 08093
(609) 853-6490
TTY: 853-7602
FAX: 853-1466

New Mexico

Independent Living
   Resource Center
4401-B Lomas Northeast
Albuquerque, NM 87110
(505) 266-5022
TTY: 266-5022
FAX: 266-5150

Southern New Mexico
   Center for IL
118 South Downtown Mall,
   Suite C
Las Cruces, NM 88001
(505) 526-5016
TTY: 526-5016
FAX: 526-1202

New Vistas
1205 Parkway Drive
Santa Fe, NM 87504
(505) 471-1001
TTY: 471-1001
FAX: 471-4427

New York

Capital District Center for Independence
845 Central Avenue
Albany, NY 12206
(518) 459-6422
TTY: 459-6422
FAX: 459-7847

ILC of Amsterdam, Inc.
12 Chestnut Street
Amsterdam, NY 12010
(518) 842-3561
TTY: 842-3593
FAX: 842-0905

Options for Independence
75 Genesee Street
Auburn, NY 13021
(315) 255–3447
TTY: 255-3447
FAX: none

Batavia Center for Independent Living
61 Swan Street
Batavia, NY 14020
(716) 343-4524
TTY: 343-4524
FAX: 343-6656

Southern Tier Independence Center
107 Chenango Street
Binghamton, NY 13901
(607) 724-2111
TTY: 724-2111
FAX: 722-5646

Bronx Independent Living Services
3525 Decatur Avenue
Bronx, NY 10467
(718) 515-2800
TTY: 515-2803
FAX: 515-2844

Brooklyn Center for Independence of the Disabled
2044 Ocean Drive, Suite B3
Brooklyn, NY 11230
(718) 998-3000
TTY: 998-7406
FAX: 998-3473

Independent Living Center of Western NY
3108 Main Street
Buffalo, NY 14214
(716) 836-0822
TTY: 836-0822
FAX: 835-3967

Native American IL Services
3108 Main Street
Buffalo, NY 14214
(716) 836-0822
TTY: 836-0822
FAX: 835-3967

SILO (Satellite Office)
3180 Express Drive South
Central Islip, NY 11722
(516) 348-0207
TTY: 348-7655
FAX: 348-0262

Access to Independence and
    Mobility
271 East First Street
Corning, NY 14830
(607) 962-8225
TTY: 962-8225
FAX: 937-5125

Glens Falls Independent
    Living Center
P.O. Box 453
25 Sherman Avenue
Glens Falls, NY 12801
(518) 792-3537
TTY: 792-0505
FAX: 792-0979

Finger Lakes Independence
    Center
609 West Clinton Street,
    Suite 112
Ithaca, NY 14850
(607) 272-2433
TTY: 272-2433
FAX: 272-0902

Queens Independent Living
    Center
140-40 Queens Blvd.
Jamaica, NY 11435
(718) 658-2526
TTY: 658-4720
FAX: 658-5295

Southwestern Independent
    Living Center
843 North Main Street, Rear
    Entrance
Jamestown, NY 14701
(716) 661-3010
TTY: 661-3012
FAX: 661-3011

Resource Center for
    Accessible Living, Inc.
602 Albany Avenue
Kingston, NY 12401
(914) 331-0541
TTY: 331-8680
FAX: 331-2076

Long Island Center for
    Independent Living
3601 Hempstead Turnpike,
    Room 312
Levittown, NY 11756
(516) 796-0144
TTY: 796-0135
FAX: 796-0529

Massena Independent
    Living Center
156 Center Street
Massena, NY 13662
(315) 764-9442
TTY: 764-9443
FAX: 764-9464

Self Initiated Living Options
    (SILO), Inc.
3241 Route 112, Bldg. 7,
    Suite 2
Medford, NY 11763
(516) 698-1310
TTY: 698-1392
FAX: 698-1367

Office for the Physically
    Challenged
1550 Franklin Avenue
Mineola, NY 11501
(516) 535-3147
TTY: 535-3108
FAX: none

Barrier Free Living
270 East Second Street
New York, NY 10009
(212) 677-6668
TTY: 677-6668
FAX: 677-2309

Center of Independence o/t
  Disabled in NY
841 Broadway, Room 205
New York, NY 10003
(212) 674-2300
TTY: 674-2300
FAX: 674-5953

Harlem Independent Living
  Center
5-15 West 125th Street
New York, NY 10027
(212) 369-2371
TTY: 369-6475
FAX: 369-9283

VISIONS
120 Wall Street, 16th Floor
New York, NY 10005
(212) 425-2255
TTY: none
FAX: 425-7114

Independent Living Center
5 Washington Terrace
Newburgh, NY 12550
(914) 565-1162
TTY: 565-1162
FAX: 565-0567

Niagara Frontier CIL, Inc.
1522 Main Street
Niagara Falls, NY 14305
(716) 284-2452
TTY: 284-2452
FAX: 284-0829

Directions in Independent
  Living
512 West State Street
Olean, NY 14760
(716) 373-4602
TTY: 373-4602
FAX: 373-4604

Catskill Center for
  Independence
P.O. Box 1247
Oneonta, NY 13820
(607) 432-8000
TTY: 432-8000
FAX: 432-6907

North Country Center for
  Independent Living
159 Margaret Street, Suite
  202
Plattsburgh, NY 12901
(518) 563-9058
TTY: 563-9058
FAX: 563-0292

Taconic Resources for
  Independence
82 Washington Street, Suite
  214
Poughkeepsie, NY 12601
(914) 452-3913
TTY: 485-8110
FAX: 485-3196

Rochester Center for
  Independent Living
758 South Avenue
Rochester, NY 14620
(716) 442-6470
TTY: 442-6470
FAX: 271-8558

Action Toward
  Independence, Inc.
RD1, Box 144C, Route 6
Slate Hill, NY 10973
(914) 355-2030
TTY: 355-2030
FAX: 355-2060

Rockland Independent
  Living Center
238 North Main Street
Spring Valley, NY 10977
(914) 426-0707
TTY: 426-1180
FAX: 426-0989

Staten Island Center for
  Independent Living, Inc.
470 Castleton Avenue
Staten Island, NY 10301
(718) 720-9016
TTY: 720-9870
FAX: 720-9664

ARISE, Inc., Center for
  Independent Living
501 East Fayette Street
Syracuse, NY 13202
(315) 472-3171
TTY: 472-3171
FAX: 472-9252

Troy Resource Center for
  Independent Living
Troy Atrium, Broadway &
  Fourth Street
Troy, NY 12180
(518) 274-0701
TTY: 274-0701
FAX: 274-7944

Resource Center for
  Independent Living
P.O. Box 210
Utica, NY 13503
(315) 797-4642
TTY: 797-5837
FAX: 797-4747

Northern Regional Center
  for Independent Living
165 Mechanic Street
Watertown, NY 13601
(315) 785-8703
TTY: 785-8703
FAX: 785-8612

Westchester County
  Independent Living
  Center
297 Knollwood Road
White Plains, NY 10607
(914) 682-3926
TTY: 682-0926
FAX: 682-8518

Westchester Disabled on the
  Move
984 North Broadway, Suite
  L-1
Yonkers, NY 10701
(914) 968-4717
TTY: 968-4717
FAX: none

Oklahoma

Green Country IL Resource
Center
4100 SE Adams Road, Suite
C-106
Bartlesville, OK 74006
(918) 335-1314
TTY: 335-1314
FAX: 333-1814

Sandra Beasley Independent
Living Center
705 South Oakwood, Suite
B-1
Enid, OK 73703
(405) 237-8508
TTY: 237-8508
FAX: 233-6403

Oklahomans for
Independent Living
321 South Third, Suite 2
McAlester, OK 74501
(918) 426-6220
TTY: 426-6220
FAX: 426-3245

Progressive Independence,
Inc.
121 North Porter
Norman, OK 73071
(405) 321-3203
TTY: 321-2942
FAX: 321-7601

Ability Resources
1724 East Eighth Street
Tulsa, OK 74104
(918) 592-1235
TTY: 592-1235
FAX: 582-3622

Oregon

Central Oregon Resources
for IL
20436 Clay Pidgeon Court
Bend, OR 97702
(541) 388-8103
TTY: none
FAX: 388-1226

HASL Independent Abilities
Center
290 Northeast C Street
Grants Pass, OR 97526
(541) 479-4275
TTY: 479-7261
FAX: 479-7261

SPOKES Unlimited
P.O. Box 7896
Klamath Falls, OR 97602
(541) 883-7547
TTY: 883-7547
FAX: 883-7547

HASL-II (Satellite)
673 Market
Medford, OR 97504
(541) 772-7820
TTY: none
FAX: none

Living Opportunities, Inc.
P.O. Box 1072
Medford, OR 97501
(541) 772-1503
TTY: none
FAX: none

Independent Living
  Resources, Inc.
4001 Northeast Halsey
Portland, OR 97282
(503) 284-3339
TTY: 284-3339
FAX: 284-3469

Pennsylvania

Lehigh Valley Center of
  Independent Living
919 South Ninth Street
Allentown, PA 18103
(215) 790-9781
TTY: 770-9801
FAX: 770-9801

CIL of Southcentral
  Pennsylvania
1501 11th Avenue,
  Mezzanine Level
Altoona, PA 16601
(814) 949-1905
TTY: 949-1912
FAX: 949-1909

CIL of Central Pennsylvania
920 Linda Lane
Camp Hill, PA 17011
(717) 731-1900
TTY: 731-1077
FAX: 731-8150

Community Resources for
  Independence
2222 Filmore Avenue
Erie, PA 16506
(814) 838-7222
TTY: 838-8115
FAX: 838-8491

Anthracite Region CIL
40 North Church Street, City
  Hall
Hazleton, PA 18201
(717) 455-9800
TTY: 455-9800
FAX: 455-1731

Liberty Resources, Inc.
One Winding Way, Suite 108
Philadelphia, PA 19131
(215) 581-0666
TTY: 581-0664
FAX: 581-0665

CIL of Southwestern PA
7110 Penn Avenue
Pittsburgh, PA 15208
(412) 371-7700
TTY: 371-6230
FAX: 371-9430

Allied Services for the
  Handicapped
475 Morgan Highway
Scranton, PA 18508
(717) 348-2221
TTY: none
FAX: 348-2256

Northeastern Pennsylvania
  Center for IL
431 Wyoming Avenue,
  Lower Level
Scranton, PA 18503
(717) 344-7211
TTY: 344-7211
FAX: 344-7218

Berks County Center for
  Independent Living
899 Penn Avenue, Suite 2
Sinking Spring, PA 19608
(610) 670-0734
TTY: 670-0734
FAX: 670-0753

Life & Independence for
  Today
503 Arch Street Extension
St. Marys, PA 15857
(814) 781-3050
TTY: 781-1917
FAX: 781-1917

Tri-County Partnership
  for Independent
  Living
69 East Beau Street
Washington, PA 15301
(412) 223-5115
TTY: 223-5115
FAX: 223-5119

Citizens for Independence &
  Access
126 Pleasant Acres Road
York, PA 17402
(717) 840-9653
TTY: 840-9753
FAX: 840-9748

Rhode Island

Blackstone Valley Center ILP
115 Manton Street
Pawtucket, RI 02861
(401) 727-0150
TTY: none
FAX: none

PARI Independent Living
   Center
Independence Square, 500
   Prospect Street
Pawtucket, RI 02860
(401) 725-1966
TTY: 725-1966
FAX: 725-2104

IN-SIGHT Independent
   Living
43 Jefferson Blvd.
Warwick, RI 02888
(401) 941-3322
TTY: none
FAX: none

Ocean State Center for
   Independent Living
59 West Shore Road
Warwick, RI 02889
(401) 738-1013
TTY: 738-1015
FAX: 738-1083

South Carolina

Disability Action Center
3126 Beltline Blvd.
Columbus, SC 29204
(803) 779-5121
TTY: 779-0949
FAX: 779-5114

South Dakota

Opportunities for IL (O.I.L.)
P.O. Box 1571, 9 Fifth
   Avenue Southeast
Aberdeen, SD 57401
(605) 626-2976
TTY: 626-2977
FAX: 626-3154

Tateya-Topa-Ho
P.O. Box 727
McLaughlin, SD 57642
(800) 513-3203
TTY: none
FAX: (701) 854-7659

Western Resources for
  disABLED Independence
36 East Chicago
Rapid City, SD 57701
(605) 394-1930
TTY: 394-1930
FAX: 394-1933

Prairie Freedom Center for
  Independent Living
301 South Garfield Avenue,
  Suite 8
Sioux Falls, SD 57104
(605) 367-5630
TTY: 367-5630
FAX: 367-5639

Prairie Freedom Center for
  IL of Yankton
413 West 15th, Suite 107
Yankton, SD 57078
(605) 668-2941
TTY: 668-2940
FAX: 668-2940

Tennessee

Independent Living Services
  Center
3641-G Brainard Road
Chattanooga, TN 37411
(615) 622-2172
TTY: 622-2172
FAX: 624-5578

Memphis Center for
  Independent Living
163 North Angelus
Memphis, TN 38104
(901) 726-6404
TTY: 726-6404
FAX: 726-6521

Texas

Panhandle Action CIL
  Skills
3608 South Washington
Amarillo, TX 79110
(806) 352-1500
TTY: 352-8630
FAX: 354-0459

Austin Resource Center for IL
5555 North Lamar, Suite J-
  125
Austin, TX 78751
(512) 467-0744
TTY: 467-0744
FAX: 467-2417

Crockett Resource Center for IL
1020 Loop 304 East
Crockett, TX 75835
(409) 544-2811
TTY: 544-7315
FAX: 544-7315

REACH of Dallas Resource Center
8625 King George Drive, Suite 210
Dallas, TX 75235
(214) 630-4796
TTY: 630-5995
FAX: 630-6390

REACH of Denton Resource Center
405 South Elm, Suite 202
Denton, TX 76201
(817) 383-1062
TTY: 383-1062
FAX: 383-2742

Disabled Ability Resource Environment
8929 Viscount, Suite 101
El Paso, TX 79925
(915) 591-0800
TTY: 591-0800
FAX: 591-3506

REACH Resource Center on IL
1205 Lake Street
Ft. Worth, TX 76102
(817) 870-9082
TTY: 870-9086
FAX: 877-1622

Houston Center for Independent Living
7000 Regency Square Blvd. Suite 160
Houston, TX 77036
(713) 974-4621
TTY: 974-4621
FAX: 974-6927

Independent Life Styles, Inc.
P.O. Box 571874
Houston, TX 77257
(713) 977-1545
TTY: none
FAX: none

LIFE Independent Living Center
1301 Broadway Street, Suite 200
Lubbock, TX 79401
(806) 749-5433
TTY: 749-5438
FAX: 749-2618

Valley Association for IL
P.O. Box 5035
McAllen, TX 78502
(210) 781-7733
TTY: 781-7733
FAX: 781-7735

A.B.L.E. Center for Independent Living
1101 Whitaker, Suite 101
Odessa, TX 79763
(915) 580-3439
TTY: 580-3439
FAX: 580-0280

San Antonio Independent Living Services
8610 Broadway, Suite 420
San Antonio, TX 78217
(512) 805-0295
TTY: 805-0295
FAX: 822-7249

Austin Resource Center for Independent Living
400 West Hopkins, Suite 101
San Marcos, TX 78666
(512) 396-5790
TTY: 396-5790
FAX: 396-5794

U.S. Territories

Samoa Center for Independent Living
Government of American Samoa
Pago Pago, AS 96799
(684) 633-1804
TTY: none
FAX: 633-2392

Centro de Vida Independiente
Apartado 1681
Hato Rey, PR 00919
(809) 753-3109
TTY: 753-1049
FAX: 758-3101

Movimiento Alcance Vida Independiente
P.O. 25277
Rio Piedras, PR 00917
(809) 758-7901
TTY: 758-0573
FAX: 758-8844

Virgin Islands Association for IL
P.O. Box 3305
Charlotte Amalie
St. Thomas, VI 00803
(809) 775-9740
TTY: 775-9750
FAX: 775-9163

Utah

OPTIONS for Independence
1095 North Main
Logan, UT 84341
(801) 753-5353
TTY: 753-5353
FAX: 753-5390

Active Re-Entry
451 South Carbon Avenue
Price, UT 84501
(801) 637-4950
TTY: 637-4950
FAX: 637-4952

Utah Independent Living
  Center, Inc.
3445 South Main Street
Salt Lake City, UT 85115
(801) 466-5565
TTY: 466-5565
FAX: 466-2363

Opportunities for
  Independent Living
515 West 300 North, Suite A
St. George, UT 84770
(801) 673-7501
TTY: 673-0178
FAX: 673-8808

Vermont

Vermont CIL (Satellite
  Office)
532 Main Street
Bennington, VT 05201
(802) 447-0574
TTY: 447-0574
FAX: 442-4052

Vermont CIL (Satellite
  Office)
230 Main Street
Brattleboro, VT 05301
(802) 254-6851
TTY: 254-8867
FAX: 254-2651

Vermont Center for
  Independent Living
11 East State Street
Montpelier, VT 05602
(802) 229-0501
TTY: 229-0501
FAX: 229-0503

Virginia

Appalachian Independence
  Center
230 Charwood Drive
Abingdon, VA 24210
(703) 628-2969
TTY: 628-4931
FAX: none

ENDependence Center of
  Northern Virginia
2111 Wilson Blvd., Suite 400
Arlington, VA 22201
(703) 525-3268
TTY: 525-3462
FAX: 525-6835

Independence Resource
  Center
201 West Main Street, Suite 8
Charlottesville, VA 22902
(804) 971-9629
TTY: 971-9629
FAX: 971-8242

Woodrow Wilson Center for
  Independent Living
Box W37 WWRC
Fisherville, VA 22939
(703) 332-7103
TTY: 332-7103
FAX: 332-7330

Peninsula Center for
  Independent Living
2021 B Cunningham Drive,
  Suite 2
Hampton, VA 23666
(804) 827-0275
TTY: 827-0275
FAX: 827-0655

ENDependence Center, Inc.
6320 North Center Drive,
  Suite 100
Norfolk, VA 23502
(804) 461-8007
TTY: 461-7527
FAX: 455-8223

Central Virginia ILC, Inc.
2900 West Broad Street
Richmond, VA 23230
(804) 353-6503
TTY: 353-6583
FAX: 358-5606

Blue Ridge Independent
  Living Center
1502-D Williamson Road,
  Northeast
Roanoke, VA 24012
(703) 342-1231
TTY: 342-1231
FAX: 342-9505

Roanoke ILC—Dept. for
  Visually Handicapped
210 Church Avenue
  Southwest, Suite B-50
Roanoke, VA 24011
(703) 982-7122
TTY: 982-7122
FAX: none

Access Independence
312 West Cork Street
Winchester, VA 22601
(703) 662-4452
TTY: 722-9693
FAX: 662-4474

Washington

Kitsap Community Action
  Program
1201 Park
Bremerton, WA 98337
(360) 377-0053
TTY: none
FAX: none

Independent Lifestyle
  Services
109 East Third, Suite 2
Ellensburg, WA 98926
(509) 962-9620
TTY: 962-9620
FAX: 962-9620

Independent Living Service
  Center of WCCD
P.O. Box 2190
Lynnwood, WA 98036
(206) 461-4574
TTY: 461-3766
FAX: 461-4570

Center for Independence
407 14th Avenue Southeast
Puyallup, WA 98372
(206) 845-5187
TTY: 848-0798
FAX: 845-5966

Epilepsy Association
  Western Washington
1306 Western Avenue, Suite
  308
Seattle, WA 98101
(206) 623-4366
TTY: none
FAX: 623-4013

Resource Center for the
  Handicapped
20150 45th Avenue
  Northeast
Seattle, WA 98155
(206) 362-2273
TTY: none
FAX: none

WA Coalition of Citizens
  with Disabilities
4649 Sunnyside North, #100
Seattle, WA 98103
(206) 461-4550
TTY: 461-3766
FAX: 461-4570

Adventures in Independence
  Development
819 South Hatch
Spokane, WA 99202
(509) 535-9696
TTY: none
FAX: none

Coalition of Responsible
  Disabled
908 North Howard, Suite
  100
Spokane, WA 99205
(509) 326-6355
TTY: 326-6355
FAX: 327-2420

Greater Lakes Independent
  Living Center
10510 Gravelly Lake Drive
  Southwest, Suite 206
Tacoma, WA 98499
(206) 581-6085
TTY: none
FAX: none

Tacoma Area Coalition for
  Individuals with
  Disabilities
6315 South 19th Street
Tacoma, WA 98466
(206) 565-9000
TTY: 565-9000
FAX: call first

Cascade Disability Resources
P.O. Box 2129
Vancouver, WA 98668
(360) 693-8819
TTY: 693-8835
FAX: 694-1242

West Virginia

Mountain State CIL (Branch
  Office)
329 Prince Street
Beckley, WV 25801
(304) 255-0122
TTY: 255-0122
FAX: 255-0157

Appalachian Center for
  Independent Living
4710 Chimney Drive, Suite C
Charleston, WV 25302
(304) 965-0376
TTY: 965-0376
FAX: 965-0377

Mountain State Centers for
  Independent Living
821 Fourth Avenue
Huntington, WV 25701
(304) 525-3324
TTY: 525-3324
FAX: 525-3360

Northern West Virginia
  Center for IL
1130 Green Bag Road
Morgantown, WV 26505
(304) 296-6091
TTY: 291-9066
FAX: 291-9071

Wisconsin

Independent Living
  Program
1506 South Oneida Street
Appleton, WI 54915
(414) 738-2644
TTY: 738-8021
FAX: 738-2679

ILP-Curative Rehabilitation
  Center
P.O. Box 8027; 2900 Curry
  Lane
Green Bay, WI 54308
(414) 468-1161
TTY: 468-1161
FAX: 468-7851

Great Rivers Independent
  Living Services
4328 Mormon Coulee Road
LaCrosse, WI 54601
(608) 787-1111
TTY: 787-1148
FAX: 787-1114

Access to Independence,
  Inc.
1310 Mendota Street
Madison, WI 53714
(608) 242-8484
TTY: 242-8485
FAX: 242-0383

CIL for Western Wisconsin,
Inc.
UW/Stout
Menomonie, WI 54751
(715) 232-2150
TTY: 232-2150
FAX: 232-5226

IL Services and Assistance
Program
5000 West National Avenue
Milwaukee, WI 53295
(414) 348-2000
TTY: none
FAX: none

Independence FIRST
600 West Virginia Street,
Suite 300
Milwaukee, WI 53204
(414) 291-7520
TTY: 291-7525
FAX: 291-7510

Society's Assets
5200 Washington Avenue,
Suite 225
Racine, WI 53406
(414) 637-9128
TTY: 637-9128
FAX: 637-8646

North Country Independent
Living
2231 Catlin Avenue
Superior, WI 54880
(715) 392-9118
TTY: 392-9118
FAX: 392-4636

Christian League for the
Handicapped
P.O. Box 948
Walworth, WI 53184
(414) 275-6131
TTY: none
FAX: none

IL Services of Northcentral
Wisconsin
1710 West Stewart Avenue
Wausau, WI 54401
(715) 842-4805
TTY: 845-3934
FAX: 845-4580

Wyoming

Wyoming IL Rehabilitation
305 West First Street
Casper, WY 82601
(307) 266-6956
TTY: 266-6956
FAX: 266-6956

Western WY Center for
Independent Living
550 Main Street, Suite 2
Lander, WY 82520
(307) 332-4889
TTY: 332-4889
FAX: 332-2491

Rehabilitation Enterprises of
  NE Wyoming
245 Broadway
Sheridan, WY 82801
(307) 672-7481
TTY: 672-7481
FAX: 674-5117

CANADA

Alberta

Calgary Association for IL
501 18th Avenue Southwest
Calgary, Alberta T2C 0C7
(403) 244-2721
TTY: none
FAX: none

British Columbia

North Shore Disability
  Resource Center
  Association
3158 Mountain Highway
Vancouver, BC V7K 2H5
(604) 985-5371
TTY: none
FAX: 985-7594

Manitoba

Independent Living
  Resource Center
201-294 Portage Avenue
Winnipeg, Manitoba R3C
  0B9
(204) 947-0194
TTY: 947-0194
FAX: none

Ontario

IL Resource Center
303 Bagot Street, Suite 202
Kingston, Ontario K7K 5W7
(613) 542-8353
TTY: none
FAX: none

ILC of Waterloo Region
3400 King Street East
Kitchener, Ontario N2A 4B2
(519) 894-8350
TTY: 894-8350
FAX: 893-2213

Daly Support Services Corp.
101-2410 Southvale Cres.
Ottawa, Ontario K1B 5K2
(613) 736-1182
TTY: none
FAX: 736-1058

Ottawa-Carleton ILC
369A Richmond Road
Ottawa, Ontario K2A 0E7
(613) 761-8082
TTY: 761-8082
FAX: 761-1082

Niagara CIL
211 Church Street
St. Catherines, Ontario L2R
  3E8
(905) 684-7111
TTY: 684-7111
FAX: 684-1199

Independent Living Center
1201 Jasper Drive, Suite B
Thunder Bay, Ontario P7B
  6R2
(807) 345-6157
TTY: 345-6157
FAX: 345-0266

Persons United for Self-Help
  NW Ont
79 North Court Street
Thunder Bay, Ontario P7A
  4T7
(807) 345-3400
TTY: none
FAX: 345-3533

CIL in Toronto
205 Richmond Street West,
  Suite 605
Toronto, Ontario M5V 1V3
(416) 599-2458
TTY: 599-5077
FAX: 599-3555

Quebec

Carrefour Adaptation
  Quebec
320 St. Joseph East, Suite 16
Quebec City, Quebec G1K,
  8G5
(418) 522-1251
TTY: none
FAX: none

Centre de Vie Autonome/
  des Basques
C.P. 1540; 589 rue Richard
Trois-Pistoles, Quebec G0L
  3K0
(418) 851-2211
TTY: none
FAX: 851-2864

Saskatchewan

South Saskatchewan
  Independent Living
  Center
1444 Broad Street
Regina, Saskatchewan S4R
  1Y9
(306) 569-3112
TTY: none
FAX: none

Appendix D

Statewide Independent Living Councils

Alabama

Mariam Witherspoon, Vice
    Chair
1000 Park Ridge Road
Fairfield, AL 35064
(205) 325-1416
TTY: none
FAX: 325-1429

Angeline Pinkard, Staff
    Person
Vocational Rehabilitation
    Services
2127 East South Blvd.
Montgomery, AL 36111
(334) 281-8780
TTY: none
FAX: none

Kris Butler, Chair
510 West Thomason Circle
Opelika, AL 36801-5499
(334) 745-3501
TTY: none
FAX: 749-5808

Within each state or province, addresses are listed alphabetically by city.

Alaska

Patrick Reinhart, Executive
  Director
Alaska State IL Council
1016 West Sixth Avenue,
  Suite 102
Anchorage, AK 99501
(907) 272-8244
TTY: 272-8244
FAX: 277-8504

James Beck, Chair
P.O. Box 508
Palmer, AK 99645
(907) 746-0228
TTY: 746-0228
FAX: 746-0229

Arizona

Rebecca Burch, Staff Liaison
Arizona Rehabilitation
  Services Administration
1789 West Jefferson, Suite
  930-A
Phoenix, AZ 85007
(602) 542-3332
TTY: none
FAX: 542-3778

Susan Molloy, Chair
HC-63 Box 7187
Snowflake, AZ 85937
(520) 536-4625
TTY: none
FAX: none

Arkansas

SILC Coordinator
523 South Louisiana Street
Little Rock, AR 72201
(501) 372-0607
TTY: 372-0607
FAX: 372-0598

Donald Frye, Chair
11684 Gim Frye Lane
Summers, AR 72769
(501) 824-4839
TTY: none
FAX: none

California

Rebecca Coleman, Assistant
Dept. Rehabilitation
  Constituent Support Unit
830 K Street, Room L3
Sacramento, CA 95814
(916) 324-3974
TTY: 445-3123
FAX: 323-0364

Michael Humphrey, Chair
Community Resources for
  Independent Living
2999 Cleveland, Suite D
Santa Rosa, CA 95403
(707) 528-2745
TTY: 528-2157
FAX: 528-9477

Colorado

Vickie Mitschler-Skoog,
  Co-Chair
21 East Las Animas
Colorado Springs, CO 80903
(719) 471-8181
TTY: 471-2076
FAX: 471-7829

Lynn Haller, Co-Chair
2829 North Avenue, Suite
  202
Grand Junction, CO 81501
(970) 241-0315
TTY: 241-8130
FAX: 241-3341

Sharon Mikrut, Program
  Director
Community Vocational and
  IL Programs
110 16th Street, Second Floor
Denver, CO 80202
(303) 620-4181
TTY: 620-4152
FAX: 620-4189

Connecticut

Anthony LaCava, Chair
CIL of Southwestern
  Connecticut
80 Ferry Blvd.
Stratford, CT 06497
(203) 378-6977
TTY: 378-3248
FAX: 375-2748

Vince Sadowski, Staff
  Liaison Consultant
1285-A Silas Deane
  Highway, Box 187
Wethersfield, CT 06109
(860) 626-0160
TTY: 626-0160
FAX: 626-0160

District of Columbia

Grey Dougan, Vice-Chair
D.C. Center for Independent
  Living
1400 Florida Avenue
  Northeast, Suite 3
Washington, DC 20002
(202) 388-0033
TTY: 388-0033
FAX: 398-3018

Don Galloway, Chair
51 N Street Northeast, Suite
  307
Washington, DC 20002
(202) 535-1903
TTY: 535-1334
FAX: 535-1558

Delaware

Larry Henderson, Chair
Independent Resources
52 Read's Way
New Castle, DE 19720
(302) 328-6704
TTY: 324-4482
FAX: 324-4481

Harriettann Litwin, Staff
  Liaison
Division of Vocational
  Rehabilitation
4425 North Market Street,
  P.O. Box 9969
Wilmington, DE 19809
(302) 761-8300
TTY: none
FAX: none

Florida

Michael Davis, Chair
Florida Independent Living
  Council
2002 Old St. Augustine
  Road, Building A
Tallahassee, FL 32399
(904) 487-3423
TTY: 487-3423
FAX: 921-7214

Georgia

Abby Shirley, Chair
75 Langley Drive
Lawrenceville, GA 30245
(770) 945-5663
TTY: none
FAX: 945-7009

Pat Puckett, Executive
    Director
SILC of Georgia, Inc.
4247 Parkview Court
Stone Mountain, GA 30085
(404) 292-6501
TTY: none
FAX: 294-9085

Hawaii

Lorraine Hirokawa, Staff
    Liaison
State Vocational
    Rehabilitation
1000 Bishop Street, Suite 605
Honolulu, HI 96813
(808) 586-5375
TTY: none
FAX: none

Nani Fife, Chair
95-114 Hiilei Place
Mililani, HI 96789
(808) 587-3850
TTY: none
FAX: 587-3858

Idaho

Kelly Buckland, Executive
    Director
Idaho SILC
P.O. Box 83720
Boise, ID 83720
(208) 334-3800
TTY: 334-3800
FAX: 334-3803

Janette Lancaster, Chair
243 Adams Street
Twin Falls, ID 83301
(208) 734-8071
TTY: 734-8071
FAX: none

Illinois

Ann Ford, Chair
DePage County Center for
  Independent Living
400 East 22nd Street, Suite
  400F
Lombard, IL 60148
(708) 916-9666
TTY: 916-9666
FAX: 916-9688

Burton Pusch, Executive
  Director
Illinois SILC
122 South Fourth Street
Springfield, IL 62701
(217) 744-7777
TTY: 744-7777
FAX: 744-7744

Indiana

Cary Kelsey, Chair
ADEC Resources for
  Independence
P.O. Box 398
Bristol, IN 46507
(219) 293-7509
TTY: none
FAX: 293-8783

Nancy Griffin, Vice Chair
Indianapolis Resource CIL
8383 Craig Street, Suite 130
Indianapolis, IN 46250
(317) 596-6440
TTY: 596-6440
FAX: 596-6446

Iowa

John Taylor, Vice-Chair
IA Radio Reading
  Information Services
2012 40th Place
Des Moines, IA 50310
(515) 243-6833
TTY: none
FAX: none

Robert Jeppeson, Chair
1024 Walnut Street
Des Moines, IA 50309
(515) 243-1742
TTY: 243-2177
FAX: 243-5385

Kansas

Gina McDonald, Chair
1423 West Crawford
Salina, KS 67401
(913) 825-2675
TTY: 825-2675
FAX: 825-7029

Shannon Jones, Executive
  Director
SILCK
700 Jackson, Suite 1003
Topeka, KS 66603
(913) 234-6990
TTY: 234-6990
FAX: 234-6651

Kentucky

Barbara Gordon, Chair
275 East Main Street
Frankfort, KY 40601
(502) 564-4448
TTY: 564-5777
FAX: 564-9010

Sarah Richardson, IL
  Program Monitor
Morehead State University
209 St. Clair Street
Frankfort, KY 40601
(502) 564-4440
TTY: 564-6742
FAX: 564-6745

Louisiana

Lyn Fontenot, Secretary
214 Clinton Street
Lafayette, LA 70501
(318) 233-1421
TTY: none
FAX: none

Jack Master, Chair
SW Louisiana ILC
3505 Fifth Avenue, Suite A-2
Lake Charles, LA 70605
(318) 477-7194
TTY: 477-7196
FAX: 477-7198

Maine

Dale Finseth, Vice-Chair
Maine Independent Living
  Services, Inc.
424 Western Avenue
Augusta, ME 04330
(207) 622-5434
TTY: 622-5434
FAX: 622-6947

Janice LaChance, Treasurer
Maine Parent Federation
P.O. Box 2067
Augusta, ME 04330
(207) 582-2504
TTY: 582-2504
FAX: none

Steve Tremblay, Chair
Alpha One CIL
127 Main Street
South Portland, ME 04106
(207) 767-2189
TTY: 767-2189
FAX: 799-8346

Maryland

Donna Lippa,
  Administrative Assistant
MD Division of
  Rehabilitation Services
2301 Argonne Drive
Baltimore, MD 21218
(410) 554-9442
TTY: 554-9442
FAX: 554-9412

Massachusetts

Andrea Schein, Executive
  Director
State Independent Living
  Council
27-43 Wormwood Street
Boston, MA 02210
(617) 727-2175
TTY: 727-2175
FAX: 727-1354

Paul Spooner, Chair
MetroWest CIL
63 Fountain Street, Suite 504
Framingham, MA 01701
(508) 875-7853
TTY: 875-7853
FAX: none

Michigan

Patricia Cudahy, Executive
   Director
Michigan SILC
3001 North Coolidge, Suite
   125
East Lansing, MI 48823
(517) 333-4254
TTY: none
FAX: 333-4244

Jean Golden, Chair
Center of the Handicapped
3815 West St. Joseph
Lansing, MI 48917
(517) 334-7830
TTY: none
FAX: 334-7849

Minnesota

Joan Harris-Stephen, Staff
   Person
MN SILC
5228 South 30th Avenue
Minneapolis, MN 55417
(612) 290-4850
TTY: 290-4852
FAX: 290-4785

William Baur, IL Manager
Dept. of Economic Security,
   Rehab Branch
390 North Robert
St. Paul, MN 55101
(612) 296-5616
TTY: none
FAX: 296-5159

Rand Stenhjem, Chair
319 North Robert
St. Paul, MN 55101
(612) 223-2167
TTY: none
FAX: 223-2153

Mississippi

Jan Cloud, Chair
15027 Lorraine Road
Biloxi, MS 39532
(601) 392-5496
TTY: none
FAX: 396-9777

Walter Blalock, IL
    Coordinator
MS Department of
    Rehabilitation Services
P.O. Box 22806
Jackson, MS 39225
(800) 443-1000
TTY: none
FAX: none

Missouri

Eugene Weathers, Jr., Vice-
    Chair
203 North Vine
Fayette, MO 65248
(816) 248-2590
TTY: none
FAX: none

Gary Moll, Director of
    Independent Living
Vocational Rehabilitation
3224 West Truman Blvd.
Jefferson City, MO 65109
(573) 526-7009
TTY: 751-0881
FAX: 751-1441

Ann Morris, Chair
Southwest Center for
    Independent Living
1856 East Cinderella
Springfield, MO 65804
(417) 886-1188
TTY: 886-1188
FAX: 886-3619

Montana

Vickie Turner, Staff Person
MT Vocational
    Rehabilitation
Box 4210
Helena, MT 59601-4210
(406) 444-2590
TTY: 444-2590
FAX: 444-3632

June Hermanson, Chair
204 Sixth Avenue East
Polson, MT 59860
(406) 883-9459
TTY: none
FAX: none

Nebraska

Vickie Davis, Administrative
  Assistant
Vocational Rehabilitation
P.O. Box 94987
Lincoln, NE 68509
(402) 471-0901
TTY: none
FAX: 471-0117

Ed Sayre, Chair
1413 East 17th Street, 1A
Scottsbluff, NE 69361
(308) 632-4423
TTY: none
FAX: none

Nevada

Paul Gowan, Staff Support
NV Vocational Rehabilitation
7111 South Stewart Street
Carson City, NV 89709
(702) 687-4452
TTY: 687-4452
FAX: 687-3292

Fred Inman, Chair
P.O. Box 955
Hawthorne, NV 89415
(702) 945-5560
TTY: none
FAX: none

New Hampshire

Eugene Gagnon, Chair
57 Regional Drive
Concord, NH 03301
(603) 271-2773
TTY: 271-2773
FAX: 271-2837

Carol Nadeau, Operational
  Director
SILC
57 Regional Drive
Concord, NH 03301
(603) 271-2773
TTY: 271-2773
FAX: 271-2837

New Jersey

Lydia Kirschenbaum, Chair
7 West Lake Drive
Montville, NJ 07045
(201) 316-6177
TTY: 316-6178
FAX: 316-6179

Tim Cronin, IL Program
  Manager
Division of Vocational
  Rehabilitation
135 East State Street, CN 398
Trenton, NJ 08625
(609) 292-9339
TTY: 292-2919
FAX: 292-8347

New Mexico

Vince Montano, Chair
1720 Louisiana Northeast,
  Suite 204
Albuquerque, NM 87110
(505) 256-3100
TTY: 256-3100
FAX: 256-3184

Linda Siegle, Staff
Resources for Change
P.O. Box 8602
Santa Fe, NM 87504
(505) 471-3563
TTY: 471-3563
FAX: 474-4071

New York

Mary Ann Williams, Vice
  Chair
One Reamer Street
Albany, NY 12205
(518) 262-5422
TTY: none
FAX: 262-5183

Douglas Usiak, Chair
Independent Living Center
3108 Main Street
Buffalo, NY 14214
(716) 836-0822
TTY: 836-0822
FAX: 835-3967

North Carolina

Butch Cook, Chair
278 Horseshoe Drive
Boone, NC 28607
(704) 264-4083
TTY: none
FAX: none

John Dalrymple, Executive
    Director
NC Independent Living
    Rehabilitation Program
P.O. Box 26053
Raleigh, NC 27611
(919) 733-5407
TTY: none
FAX: 733-1628

North Dakota

Bill Harmson, Staff Liaison
Office of Vocational
    Rehabilitation
400 East Broadway Avenue,
    Suite 303
Bismarck, ND 58502
(701) 328-3993
TTY: none
FAX: 224-3976

Jeff Frith, Chair
Rt. 1 Box 122
Devils Lake, ND 58301
(701) 662-2517
TTY: none
FAX: none

Ohio

Tim Harrington, Interim
    Executive Director
Irene M. Ward & Associates
4949 Hayden Run Road
Columbus, OH 43221
(800) 566-7788
TTY: 566-7788
FAX: 566-7788

Linda Good, Chair
219 Village Street
Hamilton, OH 45011
(513) 863-6226
TTY: none
FAX: 737-3807

Oklahoma

Mike Ward, Chair
321 South Third, Suite 2
McAlester, OK 74501
(918) 426-6220
TTY: 426-6220
FAX: none

Melinda Fruendt, Staff
OSU Wellness Center
1514 West Hall of Fame
Stillwater, OK 74078
(405) 744-5729
TTY: none
FAX: 744-7670

Oregon

Tim Holmes, Chair
P.O. Box 100
Grande Ronde, OR 97347
(503) 879-2003
TTY: none
FAX: 879-5077

Barbara Briggs, Executive
   Assistant
State Independent Living
   Council
5145 Red Prairie Road
Sheridan, OR 97378
(503) 623-0930
TTY: 623-0930
FAX: 623-1944

Pennsylvania

Denise Aiello, Co-Chair
54103 Del Laire Road
Philadelphia, PA 19114
(610) 670-7303
TTY: 670-7736
FAX: 670-7756

Joan Kester, Staff Person
899 Penn Avenue, Suite 5
Sinking Spring, PA 19608
(610) 670-7303
TTY: 670-7736
FAX: 670-7756

Michael Auer, Co-Chair
Life and Independence for
   Today
503 Arch Street Extension
St. Marys, PA 15857
(814) 781-3050
TTY: 781-1917
FAX: 781-1917

Rhode Island

Linda Dubois, Consultant
24 Manchester Street
Bristol, RI 02809
(401) 253-9617
TTY: none
FAX: 253-9617

Dorothy Hoye, Chair
250 Milton Road
Warwick, RI 02888
(401) 467-8235
TTY: none
FAX: none

South Carolina

Samuel Kaetzel, Vice-Chair
1913 Spotswood Drive
Columbus, SC 29210
(803) 798-4252
TTY: none
FAX: none

Henley McElveen, Chair
110 N. Emily Drive
Lake City, SC 29560
(803) 394-2791
TTY: none
FAX: none

Kimball Gray, Executive
  Director
SC SILC
P.O. Box 2155
West Columbia, SC 29171
(803) 822-5442
TTY: none
FAX: none

South Dakota

Shelly Pfaff, Executive
  Secretary
SD Coalition of Citizens
  with Disabilities
221 South Central Avenue,
  Suite 34A
Pierre, SD 57501
(605) 945-2207
TTY: 945-2207
FAX: none

Dick Hicks, Chair
1916 Edgewood Road
Sioux Falls, SD 57103
(605) 336-2094
TTY: none
FAX: none

Tennessee

Charlie Buck, Executive
    Director
2701-B Bellcord Avenue
Nashville, TN 37212
(615) 242-6200
TTY: none
FAX: none

Jackie Page, Chair
Howard Office
Building G-52
700 Second Avenue South
Nashville, TN 37210
(615) 862-6492
TTY: 862-6492
FAX: none

Texas

Carl Wright, Chair
P.O. Box 5368
Austin, TX 78763
(800) 235-0915
TTY: (800) 235-0915
FAX: none

Brenda Shaw,
    Administrative
    Coordinator
TX SILC
8610 Broadway, Suite 420
San Antonio, TX 78217
(800) 863-0908
TTY: none
FAX: (210) 805-9013

U.S. Territories

Peter Kolone, Chair
c/o Pete Galea'i
DVR Dept. HR
Pago Pago, AS 96799
10288-011-684-633-2336
TTY: none
FAX: none

Frank Mullen, Chair
% Dept. of Vocational
    Rehabilitation
122 ITE Plaza, Room B201
Harmon Industrial Park
Guam 96911
10288-011-646-9468
TTY: none
FAX: none

Senen Rivera Ortiz, Chair
Calle Rio, Cialitos
Suite C-20
Urb Rio Hondo
Bayamon, PR 00961
(809) 787-7322
TTY: none
FAX: none

Rebecca Diaz Rodriguez,
    Executive Director
SILC
Apartado 1681
Hato Rey, PR 00919
(809) 753-3109
TTY: 753-3101
FAX: none

Utah

Brian Dale, Executive
  Director
Utah SILC
1800 Southwest Temple,
  Suite 317-47
Salt Lake City, UT 84115
(801) 463-1592
TTY: 463-1592
FAX: 463-1683

Nancy Wagner, Chair
1800 Southwest Temple,
  Suite 317-47
Salt Lake City, UT 84115
(801) 463-1592
TTY: 463-1592
FAX: 463-1683

Vermont

Suzanne Austin, Executive
  Coordinator
SILC of Vermont
RR 1, Box 1495
Montpelier, VT 05602
(802) 229-1107
TTY: none
FAX: 229-2735

E. Ingrid Anderson,
  Co-Chair
RR 2, Box 190
Springfield, VT 05156
(802) 546-4587
TTY: none
FAX: none

Dan Gilman, Co-Chair
3 Merrick Street
Rutland, VT 05701
(802) 773-4739
TTY: none
FAX: none

Virginia

Maureen Hollowell, Chair
ENDependence Center, Inc.
6320 North Center Drive,
  Suite 100
Norfolk, VA 23502
(804) 461-8007
TTY: 461-7527
FAX: 455-8223

Jim Rothrock, Staff Person
Rothrock Group
1802 Marroit Road
Richmond, VA 23229
(804) 673-0119
TTY: none
FAX: 282-7118

Washington

Sandy Adams, Executive
  Director
State of WA, DSHS/DVR
P.O. Box 45343
Olympia, WA 98504
(360) 407-3603
TTY: 407-3603
FAX: 438-8379

Charles Grant, Chair
1527 West Tenth Street
Port Angeles, WA 98363
(360) 457-0530
TTY: none
FAX: 452-9700

West Virginia

Anne Weeks, Chair
Mountain State CIL
821 Fourth Avenue
Huntington, WV 25701
(304) 525-3324
TTY: 525-3324
FAX: 525-3362

Executive Director
WV SILC
P.O. Box 50890
Charleston, WV 25305
(800) 642-8207
TTY: none
FAX: none

Wisconsin

Deb Wisniewski, Staff
SILC-Room 1150
P.O. Box 7850
Madison, WI 53707
(608) 266-7797
TTY: none
FAX: none

Karen Hodgson, Chair
University of Wisconsin/
  Stout
Menomonie, WI 54751
(715) 232-2150
TTY: 232-2150
FAX: none

Wyoming

Darlo Koldenhoven, Staff
  Liaison
Department of Vocational
  Rehabilitation
1104 Herschler Building
Cheyenne, WY 82002
(307) 777-6841
TTY: 777-7386
FAX: 777-7155

Mike Pfaffenhauser, Chair
P.O. Box 226
Lusk, WY 82225
(307) 777-3641
TTY: none
FAX: none

Index

Page numbers followed by "f" or "t" indicate figures or tables, respectively.

Abstinence
  definition of, 151
  resuming sexual activity after, 62
Abuse
  physical, 62–63
  sexual, 63
Acceptance, of injury, 19
Accessibility, of public places, 43
Acquired immunodeficiency syndrome (AIDS), 143–144
  and anal sex, 136
  and contraceptive devices, 146
  definition of, 151
  and gays/lesbians, 147–148
  and oral sex, 146–147
Adoption, 133–134
Aggressiveness, in relationships, 41
Aging
  and changes in sexual activity, 66–67
  and problems with erections, 92
AIDS, *see* Acquired immunodeficiency syndrome
Alabama
  independent living centers in, 167
  independent living councils in, 213
Alaska
  independent living centers in, 167–168
  independent living councils in, 213
Alberta, independent living centers in, 209
Alcohol, 76
  effects on sexual activity, 75
  and sexually transmitted diseases, 145

and use of vacuum device for erections, 83
American Association of Sex Educators, Counselors, and Therapists, address, 165
American Board of Sexology, address, 166
American Congress of Rehabilitation Medicine, address, 165
American Samoa
  independent living centers in, 211
  independent living councils in, 230
Anal sex, 136
Anemia, during pregnancy, 135
Anger, after injury, 19
Anus, definition of, 151
Anxiety, definition of, 151
Appearance, *see* Body image
Arizona
  independent living centers in, 168
  independent living councils in, 214
Arkansas
  independent living centers in, 168–169
  independent living councils in, 214
Assertiveness, in relationships, 41
Autonomic dysreflexia, 5, 95–96, 110, 122
Autonomic hyperreflexia, 100
  definition of, 151
  during pregnancy, 135

Back injuries, 2
Birth control, types of, 124–127, 125f

Birth control pill, 10*f,* 124, 126
　definition of, 152
　drug interactions, 76
Bladder, 6*f,* 9*f*
Bladder accident
　definition of, 152
　during sexual activity, 104
Bladder function
　after spinal cord injury, 4–5, 20–21
　talking with partner about, 102–103
Bladder infection
　definition of, 152
　sexual activity during, 103
Body image
　definition of, 35
　expression of, 40
　improving, 36–37
Bowel, definition of, 152
Bowel accident, during sexual activity, 106–107
Bowel function
　after spinal cord injury, 4–5, 20–21
　talking with partner about, 102–103
Breast
　definition of, 152
　examination of, 132
　self-examination of, 10–11
Breast-feeding, 137
British Columbia, independent living centers in, 209

California
　independent living centers in, 169–172
　independent living councils in, 214
Canada, independent living centers in, 209–211
Catheters, 4
　placement during sex, 105
Caverject (alprostadil for injection), 152
Center for Sexual Function, address, 165
Cervical region, 1*f*
　definition of, 152
　injuries to, 2*f,* 2–3
Cervix, 10
　definition of, 152

Children, reactions to wheelchairs, 139
Chronic pain, 109–110
Cigarette smoking, effects on erections, 75
Clitoris, 8–10, 9*f,* 11, 98–99
　definition of, 152
Clothes
　appropriate for wheelchairs, 37
　shopping for, 38
Cocaine, 76
Colorado
　independent living centers in, 172–173
　independent living councils in, 214–215
Coming out, for gays/lesbians, 55–56
Community integration, 17–29
Condoms, 10*f,* 126–127
　and AIDS, 146
Confidence, after spinal cord injury, 35–36
Connecticut
　independent living centers in, 173–174
　independent living councils in, 215
Contraceptive pills, 10*f,* 124, 126
　definition of, 152
　drug interactions, 76
Contraceptives
　and acquired immunodeficiency syndrome (AIDS), 146
　types of, 124–127, 125*f*
Corpora cavernosa, 5
Counseling, 19–20
　definition of, 152
　marriage, 66
Covenant Rehabilitation Center, address, 165

Dating, *see* Relationships
Decubitus ulcers, 3–4
Delaware
　independent living centers in, 174
　independent living councils in, 215
Denial, after injury, 19
Depression
　after injury, 19

definition of, 153
effect on erections, 78
Diabetes, definition of, 153
Diaphragm, for birth control, 10f,
     126
  definition of, 153
  insertion of, 127
Dildo, definition of, 153
District of Columbia
  independent living centers in,
     208
  independent living councils in,
     230
Doctor, *see* Health care providers
Douche, 131
Drugs
  effects on sexual activity, 75–76
  for sexual arousal, 77
  and use of vacuum device for
     erections, 83
Dysfunction, definition of, 153
Dysreflexia, *see* Autonomic dys-
     reflexia

Ejaculation, 101–102
  definition of, 153
  premature, definition of, 158
  retrograde, 7
     definition of, 160
  use of vibrator for, 90
Electroejaculation, 123
  definition of, 154
Embarrassment, of health care pro-
     viders, and questions about
     sex, 23–24
Emotional orgasm, 100–101
Endocrinologist, definition of, 154
Erections
  changes with aging, 92
  and depression, 78
  lack of, 79
  medications to improve, 77
  penile implants for, 86–89
  physiology of, 5
  reflex, 79–80
  research about, 149
  and self-esteem, 78
  and smoking, 75
  types of, 79–80
  use of penis ring for, 81–82
  use of vacuum device for, 82–85
  without ejaculation, 102

Estrogen, definition of, 154
Excitement phase, of sexual
     arousal, 12–13

Fallopian tubes, definition of, 154
Fathering, 138–139
Feminine hygiene, 119–139
Fertility, 119–139
  improving chances of, 122
  male, 24–25, 121
  research about, 149–150
Florida
  independent living centers in,
     174–175
  independent living councils in,
     216
Foreskin, 5

G spot, 99, 148
Gay, definition of, 154
Gay/lesbian
  and AIDS, 147–148
  issues involved with, 55–56
  meeting partners, 42–43
Genetic counseling, 134–135
Genitals, definition of, 154
Georgia
  independent living centers in,
     176
  independent living councils in,
     216
Glans, definition of, 154
Glans penis, 5
Grieving process, after injury, 19–20
Guam, independent living councils
     in, 230
Gynecological exams, 132
Gynecologist
  definition of, 154
  finding, 26

Handicap Introductions/H.I. (Na-
     tional Computer Matching),
     address, 166
Hawaii
  independent living centers in,
     176
  independent living councils in,
     216
Head injury
  effects on sexual activity, 77
  traumatic, definition of, 162

Health care providers
  sexual activity with, 22, 28–29
  talking about sexual questions
    with, 23, 28
Heroin, 76
Herpes, 143–144
Herpes II, definition of, 155
Homosexual, *see* Gay/lesbian
Hormone replacement therapy, 69–
  70
Hormones
  imbalance, and pain during inter-
    course, 111
  to improve erections, 77
Hygiene, to prevent bladder infec-
  tions, 103
Hymen, and pain during inter-
  course, 110–111
Hyperreflexia, *see* Autonomic hyp-
  erreflexia
Hypersensitivity, 108

Idaho
  independent living centers in,
    176–177
  independent living councils in,
    217
Identity, definition of, 155
Illinois
  independent living centers in,
    177–179
  independent living councils in,
    217
Implants, penile, *see* Penile implants
Impotence, 24–25
  definition of, 155
Independence, and sexuality, 51–52
Independent living centers (ILC)
  addresses
    in Canada, 209–211
    in the United States, 167–209
  definition of, 155
  services available from, 27
Independent living councils, statewide, addresses of, 213–230
Indiana
  independent living centers in,
    179
  independent living councils in,
    217

Infertility
  definition of, 155
  male, 121
Injection program, *see* Penile injection program
Insurance coverage, for urologist
  or sex therapist, 25–26
Intercourse
  definition of, 156
  see also Sexual activity
Intrauterine device (IUD), 10*f*, 126
  definition of, 156
Iowa
  independent living centers in,
    179–180
  independent living councils in,
    218

Kansas
  independent living centers in,
    180–181
  independent living councils in,
    218
Kegel exercises, for tightening of
  vaginal muscles, 61, 148
Kentucky
  independent living centers in,
    181
  independent living councils in,
    218

Labia, 8–11, 98
  definition of, 156
Labia majora, 8–10
Labia minora, 8–10
Leg bag, placement during sex,
  104
Lesbian
  definition of, 156
  see also Gay/lesbian
Libido, definition of, 156
Louisiana
  independent living centers in,
    181–182
  independent living councils in,
    219
Love, 47
Lubrication, 110
  vaginal, lack of, 97–98
    and pain during intercourse,
      110–111

Lumbar region, 1*f*
    definition of, 156
    injuries to, 2*f*, 3

Maine
    independent living centers in,
        182–183
    independent living councils in,
        219
Male menopause, 67–68
Male superior position, definition
    of, 156
Manitoba, independent living cen-
    ters in, 209
Marijuana
    effects on sexual activity, 75
    and use of vacuum device for
        erections, 83
Marriage, 64–65
Marriage counselor, 66
Maryland
    independent living centers in,
        183
    independent living councils in,
        219
Masculinity, 52
Massachusetts
    independent living centers in,
        183–184
    independent living councils in,
        220
Masturbation, 93–94
    complications with, 94–95
    definition of, 156
    by women, 97
Medicare, coverage for urologist or
    sex therapist, 25
Medications
    effects on sexual activity, 75–76
    to improve erections, 77
Menopause
    definition of, 157
    hormone replacement therapy
        with, 69–70
    male, 67–68
    sexual activity after, 67–68
Menstrual pads, and skin irrita-
    tions, 130
Menstruation, 128–129
    definition of, 157
    hygiene during, 130

Methadone, 76
Michigan
    independent living centers in,
        184–186
    independent living councils in,
        220
Minnesota
    independent living centers in,
        186–187
    independent living councils in,
        220
Mississippi
    independent living centers in,
        187
    independent living councils in,
        221
Missouri
    independent living centers in,
        188–189
    independent living councils in,
        221
Mons veneris, 8
Montana
    independent living centers in,
        189
    independent living councils in,
        221
Mothering, 137–138
Motor skills, with spinal cord in-
    jury, 2–3
Multiple sclerosis, definition of,
    157

National Council on Independent
    Living/Access Living, ad-
    dress, 166
National Rehabilitation Center
    and Able Data, address,
    166
National Spinal Cord Association,
    address, 166
National Spinal Cord Foundation,
    for doctor referrals, 26
National Spinal Cord Injury Hot-
    line, address, 166
Nebraska
    independent living centers in,
        189–190
    independent living councils in,
        222
Neck injuries, 2

Nerve injuries
  cervical, 2f, 2–3
  lumbar, 2f, 3
  sacral, 2f, 3
  thoracic, 2f, 3
Nevada
  independent living centers in,
    190
  independent living councils in,
    222
New Hampshire
  independent living centers in,
    190
  independent living councils in,
    222
New Jersey
  independent living centers in,
    191–192
  independent living councils in,
    223
New Mexico
  independent living centers in,
    192
  independent living councils in,
    223
New York
  independent living centers in,
    192–196
  independent living councils in,
    223
Nicotine, effects on erections, 75
Nipples, definition of, 157
North Carolina
  independent living centers in,
    196
  independent living councils in,
    224
North Dakota
  independent living centers in,
    197
  independent living councils in,
    224
Nurse, see Health care providers

Ohio
  independent living centers in,
    197–198
  independent living councils in,
    224
Oklahoma
  independent living centers in,
    198–199

independent living councils in,
    225
Ontario, independent living centers
    in, 209–210
Oral sex
  and AIDS, 146–147
  definition of, 157
Oregon
  independent living centers in,
    199
  independent living councils in,
    225
Orgasms, 13–14, 99–100, 148
  definition of, 157–158
  emotional, 100–101
  multiple, 101–102
Ovaries, 9f, 10
  definition of, 158
Ovulation, 129
  definition of, 158

Pain
  chronic, 109–110
  interference with sexual activity,
    108–109
Papaverine, for erections, 89–90
  definition of, 158
Paralyzed Veterans of America, ad-
    dress, 166
Para-orgasm, 100
Paraplegia, definition of, 2
Parenting, 119–139
Parents
  discussing sex with, 54–55
  effect on development of sexual
    identity, 54
Partners, see also Relationships
  with disabilities, 44–45
  fear of rejection from, 20
  gay/lesbian, 42–43, 56
  getting pleasure from sexual ac-
    tivity, 58
  loss of interest in sex, 58–59
  meeting, 41–43
    gay/lesbian, 42–43
  role confusion of, 29
  talking about injury with, 45–46
  talking about sex with, 28, 57
Passivity, and lack of sexuality, 51–
    52
Peer counseling, 19–20, 23, 28
  definition of, 158

Pelvic exams, 132
Pelvic inflammatory disease, 126
Penile implants, 86*f*, 86–89, 87*f*
    definition of, 155
    removal of, 88–89
    side effects of, 89
    types of, 86–87
    and use of vacuum devices, 85
Penile injection program, 89–91, 90*f*
    side effects of, 91
    and use of vacuum devices, 85
Penis, 6*f*
    anatomy and function, 5
    definition of, 158
    during excitement phase, 12
    during orgasm, 14
    during plateau phase, 13
    self-examination of, 8
    size, 92–93
Penis ring, for erections, 81–82
Pennsylvania
    independent living centers in,
        199–201
    independent living councils in,
        225
Periods, *see* Pregnancy
Personal care attendant (PCA), sex-
    ual activity with, 28–29
Peyronie disease, 81
Physiatrist, definition of, 158
Physical abuse, 62–63
Planned Parenthood, address, 166
Plateau phase, of sexual arousal,
    13
PMS, *see* Premenstrual syndrome
Positions, for sex, *see* Sexual posi-
    tions
Pregnancy, 129, 133, 135
    signs of labor, 136
Premature ejaculation, definition
    of, 158
Premenstrual syndrome (PMS), 128
Pressure sores, 3–4
Priapism, 91
Prostaglandin, for erections, 89–90
Prostate, 6*f*, 7
    definition of, 158
Prostitute, hiring after spinal cord
    injury, 64
Psychiatrist, definition of, 159
Psychologist, definition of, 159
Psychotherapy, definition of, 159

Puberty, definition of, 159
Public places, accessibility of, 43
Puerto Rico
    independent living centers in,
        211
    independent living councils in,
        230

Quadriplegia
    definition of, 2
    motor function with, 2–3
Quebec, independent living centers
    in, 210

Rectum, 6*f*
Reflex erections, 79–80
Refractory period, of sexual
    arousal, 14–15
Regitine, for erections, 89–90
Rehabilitation, 17–29
    definition of, 159
Rehabilitation center, sexual activ-
    ity at, 21–22
Rejection, fear of, 20
Relationships
    importance of sex in, 57
    inadequacy fears in, 39
    issues involved in, 45
    long-term, 46
    remaining single, 53
    and self-esteem, 144–145
    starting, 41–42, 44
    see also Partners
Research on sexuality
    for men with spinal cord injury,
        149–150
    for women with spinal cord in-
        jury, 148–149
Resolution phase, of sexual
    arousal, 14–15
Retrograde ejaculation, 7
    definition of, 160
Rhode Island
    independent living centers in,
        201
    independent living councils in,
        226

Sacral region, 1*f*
    definition of, 160
    injuries to, 2*f*, 3
Sadness, after injury, 19

Saskatchewan, independent living
    centers in, 211
Scrotum, 6f, 7
    definition of, 160
    self-examination of, 8
Self-esteem, 35–36
    and abusive relationships, 62–63
    effects on erections, 78
Self-examinations
    female, 10–11
    male, 7–8
Semen, definition of, 160
Seminal fluid, definition of, 160
Sensations, 3–4
    definition of, 160
    limited, and sexual pleasure,
        107–108
Sensuality, 107
    feelings about, 52–53
Sensuality exercises, 53
Sex, see Sexual activity
Sex drive, definition of, 160
Sex Information Education Counsel
    of the United States (SIE-
    CUS), address, 165
Sex therapist, 24
    insurance coverage for, 25–26
Sexual abuse, 63
Sexual activity, 47–48
    after periods of abstinence, 62
    changes with aging, 66–67
    discussing with parents, 54–55
    for the first time, 48–49
    frequency of, 48
    high-risk, 145
    importance in relationships, 57
    improving, 60–61
    locations for, 113–114
    loss of interest in, 49–50
    pain during, 110–111
    planning and preparation for,
        112
    during pregnancy, 135
    reducing anxiety about, 112–113
    refusal of, 60
    and sexually transmitted dis-
        eases, 141–148
    talking about, 57
    time to wait after injury, 21
    various forms of, 58
    whom to ask questions about,
        23, 28

worrying about, 50–51
Sexual anatomy
    female, 8–10, 9f
    male, 5–7, 6f
Sexual arousal
    phases of, 11–15
    physical indications of, 79
Sexual development, 53–54
Sexual fantasies, 96–97
Sexual functioning, 20–21
Sexual health
    female, 10–11
    male, 7–8
Sexual identity
    changes after spinal cord injury,
        55
    development of, 53–54
Sexual partner, see Partners
Sexual positions
    for men, 116–117
    for women, 114–115
Sexual surrogate, 26–27
Sexuality, loss of, 39–40
Sexuality and Disability Training
    Center, address, 165
Sexually transmitted diseases
    (STD), 141–148
    reducing risk of, 125–127, 143–
        144
    and self-esteem, 144–145
Shopping, for clothes, 38
Smoking
    effects on erections, 75
    risks of, 124
Social security, coverage for urolo-
    gist or sex therapist, 25
Society
    reactions of, 38–40
    views on body image, 36
South Carolina
    independent living centers in,
        201
    independent living councils in,
        226
South Dakota
    independent living centers in,
        201–202
    independent living councils in,
        226
Spasticity
    definition of, 161
    during sex, 111–112

Speculum, 11
Sperm, definition of, 161
Sperm bank, 123
Spermicidal foam, 10f, 126–127
   and AIDS, 146
Spermicidal gel, 126–127
Spermicidal jelly, 10f
   and AIDS, 146
Spinal cord injury, 1f
   complete lesion, 1–2
   definition of, 161
   life expectancy with, 1
Spouse, *see* Partners
Stuffing, 80–81
Suprapubic tube, placement during
   sex, 105–106
Surgical procedures, to improve
   erections, 91–92

Tampons
   pain with, 130–131
   and skin irritations, 130
Tennessee
   independent living centers in,
      202
   independent living councils in,
      227
Testicles, 6f, 7
   definition of, 161
Testosterone, 77
   definition of, 161
Texas
   independent living centers in,
      202–203
   independent living councils in,
      227
Therapist, *see* Health care pro-
     viders
Thoracic region, 1f
   definition of, 161
   injuries to, 2f, 3
Toxic shock syndrome, 131
Transfer, into bed, 114
Transvestitism, definition of, 162
Trazodone, 77
Tubal ligation, 127

United States
   independent living centers in,
      167–208
   independent living councils in,
      213–230

United States territories
   independent living centers in,
      209
   independent living councils in,
      230
Urethra, 5, 6f, 7, 9f
   definition of, 162
Urinary tract infection, 103
   during pregnancy, 135
Urologist, 24–25
   definition of, 162
   insurance coverage for, 25–26
Utah
   independent living centers in,
      204
   independent living councils in,
      227
Uterus, 9f, 10
   definition of, 162

Vacuum device, for erections, 82–
     85, 83f–84f
   complications with, 85
   definition of, 162
   satisfaction with, 84
Vagina, 8, 9f
   definition of, 162–163
   during excitement phase, 12–
     13
   Kegel exercises for, 61, 148
   lubrication of, 97–98, 110–111
   muscle tightness of, after spinal
     cord injury, 61–62
   during orgasm, 14
   during plateau phase, 13
   self-examination of, 10–11
Vaginal discharge, 132
Vaginismus, definition of, 163
Vas deferens, 7
   definition of, 163
Vascular, definition of, 163
Vasectomy, 127
Venereal disease
   definition of, 163
   see also Sexually transmitted dis-
     eases
Venereal warts, definition of, 163
Vermont
   independent living centers in,
      204
   independent living councils in,
      228

Vibrator, 94*f*, 95
  complications with, 94–96
  use by men, 95–96
Vibratory stimulation, 122
Virgin Islands, independent living
    centers in, 211
Virginia
  independent living centers in,
    204–205
  independent living councils in,
    228
Vulva, 8, 11
  definition of, 163

Washington (state)
  independent living centers in,
    205–206
  independent living councils in,
    228
Washington, D.C.
  independent living centers in,
    208
  independent living councils in,
    230

West Virginia
  independent living centers in,
    207
  independent living councils in,
    229
Wet dreams, 97
Wheelchairs
  accessibility with, 43
  children's reactions to, 139
  finding clothing appropriate for,
    37
  sex in, 113–114
Wisconsin
  independent living centers in,
    207–208
  independent living councils in,
    229
Wyoming
  independent living centers in,
    208
  independent living councils in,
    229

Yohimbine, 77

SUNY BROCKPORT

3 2815 00799 7946

RD 594 .3 .D83 1997

Ducharme, Stanley H.

Sexuality after spinal cord
injury

DATE DUE

DEC 1 0 1999

DEC 2 1 1999

DRAKE MEMORIAL LIBRARY
WITHDRAWN
THE COLLEGE AT BROCKPORT

GAYLORD   PRINTED IN U.S.A.